# Shoes in the Bible and Walking with God

Patty Howell

CROSSLINK PUBLISHING

Shoes in the Bible and Walking with God

D CrossLink Publishing
C www.crosslinkpublishing.com

ISBN 978-1-936746-84-2

Library of Congress Control Number: 2013952149

# About the Author

Growing up as a pastor's daughter was something Patty would not change for any earthly treasure. The faith she witnessed in her mother and dad was a genuine life-shaping faith. Sermon after sermon, and Sunday school class after Sunday school class, God's Word laid a foundation in her heart that still guides her today. Jesus became her Lord and Savior at a young age, and her life has His signature written over every sorrow and joy.

Patty is the wife of Pastor Billy Howell. They have three daughters: Ashley, Brooke, and Caitlyn. The call of Patty's heart is to share God's Word in a clear manner with ladies who are struggling to understand how to study God's precious Word.

To my Lord and Savior:

My favorite place is at your feet.

To my wonderful husband, daughters, and our family:

Thank you for your encouragement.

Walking with you in this life is my sweetest earthly joy.

To all our Church families:

We "thank our God on every remembrance of you".

(Philippians 1:3)

To the Christian ladies

who have walked with me in this study:

You can tell a lot about people from their shoes, and

you each wear the shoes of your Savior beautifully!

To Gail, James, and family:

Thank you for all the typing, the Sunday meals, and

love; our feet feel at home under your table.

**To Crosslink Publishing:**

**Thank you for believing in me.**

**May God bless your ministry richly above all**

**you dream or imagine.**

# Contents

# Preface

Have you ever set your mind to study the Bible, only to find yourself confused and unable to understand what you are reading? In Acts 8:30, we read about an Ethiopian man who was reading the writings of Isaiah. As Philip came by, he asked this Ethiopian eunuch if he understood what he was reading. The eunuch replied, "How can I, except some man should guide me?" (v.31). With that response, Philip moved in to help this man understand what he was reading. Philip wanted the eunuch to understand the truth of God's Word and to see how it applied to his life. Yet more than Philip, God cared for this one soul who humbly sought his truth.

The Holy Spirit provoked Philip to go meet up with a chariot. Inside the chariot was a man who had been to the temple (to church) and was returning home. God told his servant to go out and meet this Ethiopian in the desert. As the eunuch sat in his chariot trying to comprehend the scriptures, God had Philip there to put the bread on the table so that this man could reach it. Every infant needs someone to feed them milk until they can move on to obtain meat for themselves. My heart is touched by the profound need for spiritual nurturing among Christian believers. God has called me to help make the Bread of Life reachable to those who are hungry and thirsty to understand the Word of God.

The Bible was written in a different time and out of a different culture. Many of its truths are hidden and must be searched for like gold, yet it is open to every sincere pursuer of God's truth. I believe—with a little help in breaking down the symbols of an ancient culture and applying them to your daily life—that you, dear reader, can come to understand what you read. God's Word says that his people perish for lack of knowledge (Hosea 4:6). Make up your mind today, that you will no longer be one who is confused about the scriptures, but one who will live to discover the Bible, the truth of the ages.

I'm excited to present one of several theme studies that will hopefully "connect the dots" for you in your Bible study. *Shoes in the Bible* is a study of the shoes of the scripture and the life lessons they offer on how to walk with God. In order to make the most of this study, I encourage you to consider the following guidelines:

- Begin with the chapter overviews (located in the Appendix) before each week of study.
- Pray at the beginning of each daily study asking God to give you understanding.
- Commit to complete this study. The enemy will try to discourage you.
- Pass on what you learn to others. Consider leading a group study of "Shoes in the Bible and Walking with God".

I hope you will give quality time to each chapter. I invite you to come with me now to another time and another place. Come climb over the sandy hills and walk through the deep valleys as we step into the amazing shoes of the Bible.

# Introduction

# Shoes in the Bible

D o the shoes in the Bible have spiritual meaning? Have you ever wondered why God told Moses to remove his shoes? Have you ever pondered the fact that Boaz claimed Ruth with a simple shoe, or ever contemplated the significance of Paul shaking the dust off his soul-winning sandals? Surprisingly, there are "soul truths" tied up in the shoes of God's Word! The scripture's shoes can help us learn many valuable lessons about how to walk with God.

It is my prayer that this study through God's Word will help you to understand the true meaning of walking in God's ways. David prayed in Psalms 25:4, "Show me thy ways, O Lord; teach me thy paths." God's Word tells us that his ways are "higher than our ways," so then how are we to find the ways of God? First, we must begin as David did. We should ask God to show us his ways. Although it may take time, we can be assured that his answers will always come, and they will always come through his Word. Next, as we seek his wisdom in his Word, we will see connecting themes that help us understand his ways. Many times in the scripture, God uses subjects and symbols to reveal His ways. One way to study the Word of God is by subject studies. Tracing key words or cultural symbols throughout the scriptures can shed light on lessons and patterns. In this particular study, we will follow the symbol of the shoe in the Bible. We will observe great people of God and what they stood upon. Think about it, what better way to learn of one's ways than by observing his walk and the testimony of his shoes. As we follow the path of shoes in the scripture, we will find a trail that leads us to the ways of God: from grace to worship, from worship to conquest, from conquest to covenant, from covenant to fellowship, from fellowship to ministry, and from ministry to the shoes of the Savior.

Shoes in the Bible have something to teach us. Throughout the Word of God, scriptural symbols personify the culture of the children of Israel. Many scholars have worked hard to establish time lines of the Bible text, and importantly so, for it helps us realize that God does all thing in the fullness of His timing. Others have studied much about the language of God's chosen people, and rightly so, for it has a unique blessing. Let us now labor, too, in a search to understand the ancient cultural symbols of God's Word. This study will undertake the revealing of one Biblical symbol, the shoe, and its significant worth to God's people.

Shoes of the Bible can serve to represent our Christian walk, and studying them can help with our everyday Christian life. The believer's spiritual closet should be well equipped with shoes fit for all occasions of the kingdom. First, we need the ruby red shoes of grace. And, of course, every soul would delight in the slippers of worship. We simply must have our sturdy boots for warfare, as well as wedding shoes for those special occasions. Walking shoes are an everyday need, and every Christian needs a quality pair. Servant's shoes are needed, too, so that we can follow our Lord as he leads us to take shoes of mercy to the unshod travelers. Finally, we will want to finish our earthly walk with shoes like those of the Savior. If we are wise, we will take time to shod ourselves with these amazing shoes of scriptures. Wonderful lessons are buried in the ancient symbols of God's Word. Our life in modern times can be helped by the shoes of antiquity. Treasures beyond our imagination await us. With this in mind, let's take up our tools and do some excavating. There is no better place to begin than Eden, and that is exactly where we will begin our search. Look! Over here! I see something near the garden, and…it looks like…a shoe!

# WEEK ONE

## Shoes of Grace

# Day One

## No Shoes Required

"And God saw every thing he had made,
and, behold, it was very good."
Genesis 1:31

As we enter the Word of God through the front door of Eden, we look into a beautiful world. Considering the fact that we have never known what unflawed beauty is like, it is hard to imagine how wondrous Eden really was. We have never had one day, hour, or moment in which everything around us was without sin. Yet Adam and Eve knew what it was like to live in a pure world. They were sinless people living in a sinless world. All was fresh and new. Everything was GOOD! Look at that word for a moment—GOOD. Note that it is just one letter away from GOD. Perhaps that is to reflect the truth that anything truly good is a work of God. Amazingly, God is so good that He even works what we call bad in our life for good. III John 1:11 says, "He that doeth good is of God." The first man and woman were "good." They lived in perfect harmony with each other and with God. Each day, God came to walk with his children, and what a glorious time they must have had! They shared heart-to-heart talks and unbroken fellowship with one another. They had complete open communion with the holy God of the universe. There was no need to stand clothed with heavily decorated priestly robes that helped fogged memories to remember God's holiness. No tedious washings or ongoing rituals had to be followed to approach the Almighty Creator. Most importantly, there were no sinful thoughts to distract man's focus from God's glory. Adam and Eve had an unhindered walk with God. They didn't have to wrap their bodies due to shame or cover their feet due to danger of harm. They had a pure standing before God. No covering was needed physically, emotionally, or spiritually. As we enter our first day of study, I want you to contemplate a question. What was it like within a flawless world where no shoes were required? With this in mind, let's take some time to imagine what Eden was like before sin.

In Genesis chapter 1, scripture tells us that God created all that man would need and proclaimed it all to be "good" (Gen. 1:10, 12, 18, 21, 25). Notice, however, that on the sixth day, after He created Adam and Eve and completed His work, He proclaimed it to be "very good." Look up the definition for *good* and write it below.

Good: _____

_____

_____

Now list some synonyms (words with similar meanings) for the word "good."

_____

_____

In your own words, describe Eden.

_____

_____

Was your description of "good" one that described a lack of evil? Mine was. How about your description of Eden, was it a picture void of sin and harm? It is hard to define "good" apart from contrasting it with "evil," isn't it? Why is this? It is due to the fact that we live in a fallen world, and, for now, we are in the realm of the knowledge of good and evil. However, Adam and Eve knew what good meant apart from evil. They had a walk with their Creator that was void of any fruition of sin. We can only imagine what the *"very good"* life of Eden was like, but let's do just that. Let's take some time to imagine life with no sin: no anger, no greed, no gossip, no competition, no condemnation, no stealing, and no killing. Imagine life with not even one negative thought crossing your mind. Sounds hard to imagine, doesn't it? Let's attempt it anyway. Come and journey with me back to Eden as we consider a life with "no shoes required."

### No Shoes Required

To begin with, the Garden of Eden was beautiful; it was every vacation paradise you've ever dreamed of. God had placed Adam and Eve in the most beautiful garden full of life and splendor. Perfectly planned and designed by the Creator, it was full of treasures. Have you ever looked closely at the biblical portrait of Eden?

Read Genesis 2:8–14.

Consider the wonders of Eden. List some of the features of this garden.

_____, _____, _____

_____, _____, _____

Did you notice the beautiful rivers? Did you consider the untainted beauty and abundance of life in Eden? What kinds of precious stones did you notice? There were, of course, the wondrous trees of Eden as well, with their branches ripe with fruit. Did you list those? If not, take a moment to write down anything you might have missed.

---

Second, let's notice in Genesis 1:31, and Genesis 2:1-6 that the earth was a safe place to live during the days of Eden—no threatening weather, not even rain. Genesis 2:5–6 tells us that God had "not caused it to rain," but that a mist went up from the ground to water the earth. Can you imagine life before watching the seven-day forecast or conversations without discussing the weather? Was there even a need for a tent of dwelling or a house before sin? There was no dangerous wildlife, and very possibly no shelter was required. All was safe before sin.

Describe a place where you feel safe. What aspects of your secret place help you feel protected?

---

You know, if we think about it, we are all trying to get back there (to a safe place), aren't we? The problem is: we carry sin with us, and the only true safe place is in the sinless person of Jesus Christ. We busy our days trying to find, buy, and build "safe places," such as, a quiet place, a better job, a larger home with a good fence, a nicer car to get away from it all, or a more fulfilling relationship that helps us "find ourselves." Sadly, some people even resort to desperate places of escape in ways such as alcohol and drugs. However, there is hope for the troubled soul. There is a place of quiet rest and beauty far more perfect than Eden, and that place is found in a personal relationship with Jesus Christ. You don't get there by tapping your red slippers in Oz; you go there by putting on the ruby red coverings of grace provided for us at the cross of Mt. Calvary. No shoes were required in Eden; it was a safe place. Thanks to the grace offered by God, we have a better feeling than going barefoot in Eden; we can put on the eternal shoes of grace.

### The Calm "Wildlife" of Eden

Now, let's picture the awe of Eden. Consider the beautiful but gentle "wildlife" of Eden.

Read Genesis 2:19–20.

Consider the thought that instead of going to the zoo, God had the zoo come to Adam. As verse 20 describes, every creature—cattle, birds, and every beast of the field—came to Adam to be named. Notice that Adam had full dominion over the animals. In our day and time, we are confined to the viewing of wild animals through the scope of a television video or through the chains of a secured cage, but Adam could pet the tiger and see the lion walk with the lamb! Have you ever imagined Eden full of wildlife before it was "wild"? Most of the artwork we see of Adam and Eve in the garden displays the couple together with maybe some trees and shrubs, but there were friendly animals around them as well. Adam and Eve must have been constantly mesmerized by the handiwork of God! As Adam observed the animals, he carefully took time to name them according to his liking. The first man and woman were constantly able to observe God's exciting creativity in the characteristics of each mammal, reptile, amphibian, bird, fish, and invertebrate. Everything in God's wonderful creation reflected some aspect of his glory—something "good." King Solomon, among his many proverbs, took time to be still and write about God's amazing creations. He observed the ant and declared her to be among God's most industrious creatures. Israel's king also gave tribute to the spider, considering how "she takes hold with her hands and is king's palaces" (Proverbs 30:28). Take a moment to think on the beauty of Eden with its garden full of amazing creatures, all safe and approachable, but hold on just a second before you do. Maybe we should do some desensitization first. As you think back to Eden, remember spiders didn't bite, snakes didn't strike, and lions didn't maul. Now go ahead, imagine a safe Eden with every kind of beautiful tame life. It makes you think of heaven, doesn't it? What beautiful scenes of the outdoors reflect God's creativity to you?

---

## The First Wedding

Finally, let's complete our look into the garden by observing one more scene—the first wedding. Take a few moments to read Genesis 2:20b–25. Be ready to describe what you observe in the first pattern of marriage.

What significant truths stand out to you about this first, God-ordained marriage?

_____

_____

I'm sure you had some very insightful findings, and I wish I could peek in your notes.

We see several important lessons in the joining of the first man and woman. First, we see that the first marriage was brought together by God. Second, the first marriage called for sacrifice. If you are like me, you are wondering, *Why was a sacrifice required before sin? Why did God choose to create woman by taking something from man?* Maybe it was to show that a union of man and wife requires full commitment. Consider the commitment that Christ has to each born-again believer.

Our marriage is to reflect the depths of His love, a Christlike love with unconditional and undying commitment. It was a love that would cost something close to Adam's heart. The first marriage was based on a sacrifice and was altogether pure and intimate.

The first man and woman were brought together by the divine hand of God, as God literally took a part of Adam to form Eve. It would cost Adam some things. A sacrifice was necessary in all areas of man's being: physically, emotionally, and spiritually. Adam would pass these important instructions of marital union onto his sons in years to come. God gave the instructions here in Genesis 2:24—that when a man and woman come together, they are to "leave" their parents and "cleave" to their mate. Let's look a little deeper here. In all actuality, Adam and Eve were joined by God. God points out physical, spiritual, and emotional union by declaring "the two shall be one" (Gen. 2:24). In other words, God was strongly ordaining the message of sacrifice and full commitment.

Let's go a little deeper on this point that a part of Adam was used to form Eve. What a beautiful picture of godly union. What an amazing Creator! A bone from Adam was used to knit the bones of Eve. I recently read that the rib bone is the only bone in the human body that does not only repair itself, but it also has the ability to regenerate or grow back! [1] Think about it, bones contain marrow, and marrow contains blood. Adam's blood was bound in his rib bone, and that bone would become the life-giving seed used to form Eve. What once flowed through his heart would now help to form hers. What a beautiful picture of how the blood of Christ gives us life. As Leviticus 17:11 tells us, "Life of the flesh is in the blood." Adam's bone with its marrow and blood was used to bring Eve to life. It is clear here to see that God joined the first man and wife by way of a sacrifice from the husband.

What else was in that choice to form woman from the rib bone of the man? I wonder if Adam's rib was to be a symbolic lesson for the woman as well. We learn in our biology classes that the role of the rib cage is to protect the heart and other vital organs. Was God relaying a message to his daughters in this act of his creation? Truly, as helpmeets, our role is to be a strong haven for our husbands. We are to constantly put a hedge of protection up for them by way of our prayers and our encouragement. Just as the rib is vitally important in helping the heart to carry out its best functions, we are to do our best to make sure that the strength of our husband's heart is protected. The words and actions of us women have enormous effects. Our job is to help our husband, to encourage and build up. This explains Satan's constant agenda to have us tear one another down by nagging and complaining instead of building one another up. A broken and wounded rib needs to be repaired. Otherwise it could puncture the lungs and take the very breath out of a body. The role of the rib is to guard the heart. I don't know about you, but I am getting the idea that I should do a lot less "ribbing" and just be more of a "rib." A lot less elbow to the ribs, and a lot more prayers to surround the hearts of our husbands are needed, are they not?

After all, our role is to be a helpmeet, right? Right! God joined man and woman, and marriage requires a sacrifice from the wife.

The first union of man and woman was the crowning finish of God's creation. Under the canopy of his love, man and woman's Creator God sealed the marriage commitment in their hearts. Quietly, beautifully, and simply, they were joined. Man and woman were one, joined: bone to bone, companion to companion, leader to helpmeet, friend to friend, and rib to heart, together in beauty and simplicity. I hope you have a well-developed mental picture now of Eden prior to sin's deadly mark of destruction. Keep in mind what we have learned; you will need it later.

In conclusion, we see the pre-sin garden scene as the most beautiful and simple backdrop of the first wedding. It was beautiful because it was absolutely pure. Adam and Eve were "not ashamed." No wedding shoes were required. Eve stood upon a holy foundation. Eve didn't even have to wear white. There was no symbolic white gown needed to show purity. She had never been dirty! She was altogether prepared. Simply put, Eve was created PURE. Creation's first wedding was good, very good. The first union by wedding was not only full of beautiful purity, but it was also complete with a beauty of simplicity. It was simple in that it needed no extravagance. God's Word joined the first man and wife, and his glorious creation was the adornment. Adam and Eve were married under the beautiful canopy of creation. Their Creator Father had draped his handiwork above them with a banner of love. Interestingly, Jewish weddings are still performed under canopies or chuppahs in this day and time. I wonder if those ceremonies have any desire to reflect the simple beauty of the first wedding in the garden. Whether or not they do, we need to remember that God designed the first wedding to be ultimately pure and beautifully simple.

The second chapter of Genesis closes with Adam and Eve walking in perfect peace (*"naked and unashamed"*). There was no fear, no guilt, or disagreements—can you imagine? Everything was "very good"! They had a flawless life, walking together, and together walking with God. Have you ever really considered the fact that they needed no covering? No covering for soul, spirit, or body? No guilt, no shame, no sorrow, and no sin? They needed no covering for their bodies, their souls, or their other "soles." No shoes required! No shoes were needed for protection, for there were no thorns to pierce their tender feet, no poisonous plants or creatures to threaten their paths. Their feet were not at all vulnerable; they could simply enjoy the bliss of being barefoot and blessed. Adam and Eve could walk and run all over God's tender creation without limit and without worry, but then...we come to Genesis 3, and everything changes. We will take a closer look in our next lesson at what exactly happened to bring about the need for the first shoes in the Bible. We will see that Eve chose to step into some shoes when she needed none. She chose the black shoes of sin and flesh. Upon her devastating choice to disobey, she could no longer walk with God. She became dressed in black. Mr. and Mrs. Adam would need a redemptive covering in exchange for the sinful shoes they had chosen to buy. Thankfully, God would provide a covering. Shoes of grace would be required to restore man's spiritual walk with an all-holy God, and God would pay the price.

**Reflect on today's study. What thought stood out in your mind?**

_____

_____

_____

_____

_____

_____

_____

_____

_____

_____

**Pray and ask God to show you what He wants you to do with the truth He has revealed to you today.**

# Day Two

# The High Heels of Low Living

"And when the woman saw that the tree was good for food, and that it was pleasant to the eyes, and a tree to be desired to make one wise, she took of the fruit thereof, and did eat, and gave also unto her husband with her; and he did eat." Genesis 3:6

Isn't it fun to hear how a couple first met? A friend once told us of his first meeting with his wife. He explained that she was from the BACKWOODS. Actually, he said she lived so far back in the woods that she came out wearing only one shoe!

*"Honey, what happened?"* he asked. *"Did you lose a shoe?"*

*"No,"* she replied. *"I found one."*

We have enjoyed that joke, yet, seriously, that was my state when Christ came to me. There I was, undone and standing in the filthy shoe of the flesh. I entered this world like every other human being—born with a sinful nature. Romans 3:23 states, "For all have sinned, and come short of the glory of God." We all stand in the shoe of the flesh wrapped around a darkened soul. Our laces are knotted, and we are all tied up with selfish desires and with our tongues loose and corrupt. That was the case for the first man and woman as well. After their choice to sin, they hid themselves. They knew they were standing in the filth of the flesh, and they knew they were undone.

15

How does God's Word define sin? Read James 4:17.

_____

_____

_____

Adam and Eve had been informed about the consequences of sin. God told them what was right to do. They knew how to *"do good,"* and they *"did it not."* Upon their decision to sin, Adam and Eve no longer stood in purity and freedom awaiting their daily walk with God in the cool of the day. Shame of sin separated them from their Creator. They covered themselves with an apron made from fig leaves, and, as we can guess, that did a very poor job of covering. The first man and woman stood in what they could piece together. As mentioned in the previous illustration, they were like the woman with one shoe, "one-shoers"—unfit, broken, and undone. Adam and Eve were now sinful people living in corrupt bodies. Sin had separated them from joy and peace; sin had sentenced them to spiritual and physical death; and sin had severed their ability to walk with God. Instead of running to meet God in the cool of the day, they hid. God's perfect and beautiful creation was now marred and corrupt. Let's take a closer look at exactly what happened to bring about man's first step into sin and low living.

Genesis 3:1 reads, "Now the serpent was more subtle than any beast of the field which the Lord God made." Note here in Genesis

3:1 that Satan had taken time to plan Eve's "trip up," and he was going for the heel. The enemy had chosen the wisest and most subtle creature with which to scheme. In Matthew 10:16, the scripture calls the serpent "wise." Satan wanted his sly approach to be brought about ever so carefully (nothing to startle). In his own scheming ways, Satan led the serpent to carry out his evil endeavors. Surely, the serpent had been led to tread on forbidden ground, because in the aftermath, he too is punished, along with the man and the woman. By his natural instincts, the serpent should have been submitting to the authority of God and man, yet he is used instead to forge Satan's wicked plan of rebellion.

We see evidence in Genesis 3:1–5 that the serpent, moved by Satan, "beguiled" Eve. And what did our all-time enemy begin with? He began with the pitfall of gossip. *"Gossip,"* you ask, *"in Genesis?"* Yes, gossip, my friends, and the slanderous words which Eve listened to were against her Almighty Creator. Through the serpent, Satan whispered curious questions. He then continued with accusations about God. You know how it goes. First, there is a quick glance by the gossiper to make sure the coast is clear. Then there is the hand raised to cover the mouth. Next the gossiper continues with a slow downward lean and sly approach to the ear canal. From there, it's on, and thus comes the scheming questions and subtle accusations. We see the questioning in Genesis 3:1(b): *"Yea, hath God said, Ye shall not eat of every tree...?"* This question is followed by the accusation in Genesis

3:4–5: "And the serpent said unto the woman, *Ye shall not surely die: for God doth know that in the day ye eat thereof, then your eyes shall be opened...."* Let's stop there for a moment. Satan is obviously calling God a liar, and Eve is listening! He uses his infamous lines that "God is holding out on her" and "not giving her all that she deserves." Can you imagine the sales pitch here? It was one so enticing that it would convince Eve to give up peace and purity for the filthy stench of sin. With the sugar of slander, Satan ever so slyly urged Eve to step toward the high heels of low living.

Continuing with the remaining part of Genesis 3:5, Satan decides to further display these shiny black heels of pride—"*ye shall be as gods, knowing good and evil,*" he assures. In the next verse (6), we see Eve take her beautiful innocent feet and step into the wicked heels of low living. "When the woman <u>saw</u> that the tree was good for food, and that it was pleasant to the eyes, and a tree to be desired to make one wise, she <u>took</u> of the fruit thereof, and <u>did eat</u>." Proud thoughts of being exalted, talk of gaining "more" by her own self effort, and discovering something better (that God was supposedly hiding)—these were the "promises" Satan set forth in the serpent's sugar-coated gossip. There seemed to be something alluring about the forbidden; these shiny black heels seemed magnetically appealing.

The high heels of low living were put on there in Eden by the touching and tasting of forbidden fruit. One moment's pleasure exchanged for generations of guilt, pain, sorrow, and death. We are still bearing the fruit of Eve's "fruit," are we not? It wasn't presented as it really was. It never is. Eve saw "possibility." She saw self glory. She imagined greener fields than Eden. Sound crazy? Think of how many times a day we fall for the high heels of low living. James 1:14 warns us that we are each tempted as we are "led astray by our own lust." After our lust comes to fruition, it brings death, just as it did for Adam and Eve. Sin is enticing. We all have some sort of shoes of the flesh that draws us to step in and walk a little taller.

Look over the following scenarios of forbidden fruits that Satan, the flesh, and the world all offer us in a day. Consider how we are led away to the point of touching then tasting these curse-filled "dainties." Take a few moments to reflect on some high heels of low living that have enticed you. We will look at the course of a daily routine to see it more clearly. Now stay with me, we are going to begin our day as the Jew (6:00 the evening before). Note: that is when our battle really begins, isn't it—the day before.

To set the stage: Just as Eve fell first to the lust of the flesh, lust of the eyes, and the pride of life, that is where we often begin our descent as well. During a normal day, we strive to obtain worldly things due to our fleshly pride. In our pursuit to gain more than God has given, we give in to being unthankful and discontent. Being overwhelmed with our overburdened pursuits, the enemy sees ample opportunity to come and offer an extra load at the closing of our day.

It's now 6:00 p.m. You are tired and weak. Hunger calls, and you have two choices:

1) Push yourself to cook a healthy home-cooked meal;
2) Give in to a quick, unhealthy and quilt-ridden fast-food dinner again. Thus begins your evening. You then face the mountain of evening chores: cleaning house, laundry, preparations for the next day. That is when the enemy presents the following *platforms to your frazzled day....

*While you are feeling fatigue and anxiety, Satan whispers ...
*"You will never get all of this done."*

*Then, in your exhaustion and frustration, Satan builds the case ...
*"You are doing a horrible job."*

* During this time when you are vulnerable, he brings up past hurts...
*"They treated you wrong,"*

*Now, in your anger, Satan continues ...
*"You need to stand up for yourself."*

* In the middle of complaining, nagging, and arguing, Satan continues ...
*"You must get your point across; you were right!"*

*You know that <u>harboring unforgiveness</u> is wrong, yet you choose to remain in <u>guilt</u>, while <u>your own mind condemns you</u> …

*"What a great Christian you are! You have blown it again!"*

*<u>Discouragement</u> follows, and your own mind continues …

*"You can't do anything right, just go to bed and forget it all."*

*The next morning, <u>procrastination</u> seems to be the next step, and your mind decides to put things off,

*"I'm not ready to face all this again, I will stay here a little longer; I am so tired."*

*When you finally do get going, you depend on <u>self-reliance.</u> (Beginning your day seeking your kingdom instead of His Kingdom, you fly into a busy morning, rushing into your day without asking for strength or guidance.)

*Next, in a weakened, self-reliant mindset, the <u>outside temptations</u> bombard us, and the world overbearingly calls out with its sales call to come and try on the high heels of low living.

*"You look so good in that. …"*

*<u>Advertisements</u> call out to our greed:

*"This would make you happy. …" "Get it now. …"*

*<u>Regret</u> ultimately follows and the flesh, the world, and the devil leave you <u>guilt-ridden</u>.

Lust of the flesh, eyes, and pride allure you (tempting you to indulge yourself with the luxuries of life without discretion or discipline). The need to wait on God to provide your needs and desires is hidden by a merciless enemy.

What does the Bible teach us in I John 2:16 about what appeals to man?

Take time to read this verse and fill in the blanks that follow.

Lust of the_____, lust of the _____, and the _____ of life.

Most of our days are full of faults and errors: are they not? We struggle with temptation, discouragements, dissatisfaction, and failure. We stumble and fall. The road of life is full of danger. Each day, worldly enticements, fleshly lusts, and traps of our enemy line our pathways. We need coverings for our feet, seeing that we walk about on a minefield of death. It is no wonder Paul tells us to be shod with the gospel of peace (Ephesians 6:15). Everything around us tries to steal our peace. Since that first steady glare at the forbidden fruit, the enemy has been at our heels. Just as he was after Eve's peace of mind, he is after ours as well. Due to her choice to sin, Eve was driven away from the Garden of Eden where she had known everything as "very good." She was then forced to abide outside the garden where the surroundings were very bad. Eve had the perfect walk. She needed no shoes, but she chose to step into the high heels of low living.

Satan has a way of making sin look appealing. He dresses it up in a cover of gold. It sparkles and shines and before we realize it, we are walking in the high heels of low living, and the guilt trip is on. We all have fallen for his sales pitch at one time or another. Thank God for his tender grace that brings us home, washes our feet, and offers us an opportunity to exchange our worn out shoes for shoes of grace.

# Day Three

# Guilty Feet Don't Walk with God

"And they heard the voice of the Lord
walking in the garden in the cool of the day: and Adam and his wife
hid themselves from the presence of the Lord God
amongst the trees of the garden." Genesis 3:8

Moving on to Genesis 3:3, we see that not only did God warn Eve not to eat of the tree of knowledge of good and evil, but He also said not to touch it—lest she die. "But of the fruit of the tree which is in the midst of the garden. God hath said, ye shall not eat of it, neither shall ye touch it, lest ye die" (Genesis 3:3). Sadly, Eve did look, and Eve did touch. She could have stopped at the look; she could have turned away, yet she continued. We don't know if the first woman came to gaze upon the forbidden tree by her own curiosity, or if the serpent enticingly led her there. However, we do know that the few seconds she chose to doubt God was all that the enemy needed to turn her aside. We should take notice from these tactics, friends, for how quickly we too can step aside. Satan is looking and waiting patiently for a few seconds to turn our foot from the narrow way. He plans long and hard to lead us astray in just a few moments. The great enemy of our soul takes time to lay his golden trap that will engulf us in instant filth. We must take time to learn how to resist him. Many men and women have fallen prey to his wooing. No wonder Paul wrote to warn us to stay far away from evil. In I Thessalonians 5:22, he penned, "Abstain from all <u>appearance</u> of evil." Paul knew that sin brings a separated walk, and that guilty feet don't walk with God.

How is sin progressive? In other words, does one sin lead to another? Read Genesis 3:6-13. Did Eve immediately fall down and repent with bitter tears after she had disobeyed her perfect Creator? Sadly, she did not.

Write down any progression of sin that you notice in these verses.

_____

_____

_____

You saw it, didn't you: sin, guilt, hiding, blaming? One wrong thought unchecked led to a downward spiral. One step in the wrong direction led to another, then another. Sin is progressive, and repentance is the only key to stop its deadly pull. Each step we take should be guarded and guarded well. For where our feet step, others follow. We need to heed the first warning. When God told Adam and Eve not to eat or touch the forbidden fruit, there were a lot of underlying checkpoints that came with keeping that rule. Eve missed some checkpoints. We can take some lessons from Eve in remembering to guard our steps. Look at the following chart of checkpoints. After studying it for a while, keep it in mind the next few days in order to evaluate your walk with God. Ask God to reveal any level of straying from His ways.

> A stronghold begins by one ungodly thought, excused and unchecked.

## DAILY CHECKPOINTS IN OUR WALK WITH GOD:

1.  Am I **content**? Do I give thanks in everything?
    (I Thess.5:18)
    *   Lack of God Contentment will result in
        Sarcasm (Grumbling)

2.  Am I **cautious**? Do I discern what is good from evil?
    (I Thess.5:21)
    *   Touching evil will lead to
        Separation (Greed)

3.  Are my thoughts **clean**? Do I run away from the sight of evil? (I Thess.5:22)
    *   Taking in evil will bring about a lack of fellowship.
        Stain (Guilt)

4. Am I **conscientious**? Do I quickly confess sin to God? (I John 1:9)

- Covering evil leaves you with

  Sorrow (Grief)

5. Am I **caring**? Do I decide to resolve differences immediately?

- Holding onto sin is pride that gives root to a

  Stronghold (Grudge)

God had pictured the magnetism and downward progression of sin in his warning—*"Don't eat or touch it"*—lest you die. In Genesis 3:6, we see that the first woman not only saw the forbidden fruit, but she also took it, ate it, and then gave it to her husband, but we can't stop there. She also hid from God and blamed the serpent. That's how the flesh responds to sin. The flesh progressively pulls the individual into a pit of ongoing corruption, and guilty feet don't walk with God. They cannot. Their guilty path has them headed in the opposite direction. No wonder we are given the question, "How can two walk together unless they agree?" (Amos 3:3). They cannot, and will not.

Consider the times you have sinned against God.

How distant did you feel?

What lies did Satan put into your mind about God?

Did the enemy draw you away with promises of "better" and the temptation to make things happen in your own strength?

Did you take the bait and travel to the tree of self-gained wisdom?

Did he then make you feel ashamed to be in God's presence?

Finally, did all of this mound into a fear of God and an anger with others?

Look back over the previous chart of daily checkpoints and warnings, where do you see yourself in comparison to the items listed?

_____

_____

_____

Take a moment to write out James 4:8. _____

_____

_____

Be encouraged that as you draw near to God, God will draw near to you.

How is your daily walk with God? Keep a check on how close you feel to your Creator. Satan will try time and again to draw you away and isolate you. He thrives on schemes that sever your supports. Once he has talked you into pulling away from God and those closest to you, he attempts to entangle you with guilt. His schemes include fear and torture. It is just his way. Maybe this would be a good time for a real-life illustration.

## "WRONG LEADS TO WRONG"

He had it all, a close relationship with God, a beautiful home, an esteemed position, then one day he left his thoughts unguarded. He decided to take some time off from work and let the other men handle the problems for the time being. He would still be on call if they needed anything. During his idle break, he knew of another who would be home as well: his neighbor's wife. To make a long story short, he contacted her, and she responded. The idle day ended up with an unexpected pregnancy. Something had to be done, and fast! The guilty party (we'll call him Jesse Jr.) called for his neighbor to take time off from work to be with his wife. Jesse could do this since he was his neighbor's boss. However, the neighbor refused to come home from work and enjoy leisure time while all the other guys carried the load. At this point, Jesse was really desperate and chose to go to more extreme measures. Jesse contacted one of his dedicated employees and made plans to do away with the neighbor and cover his guilty tracks. The employee carried out the assignment. He manipulated events that would bring about the death of the husband. Jesse thought he was free from the scenario until the pastor came by to talk with Jesse. As the pastor spoke with Jesse, he pointed out his sin. He described the heartless sins one after another: apathy, adultery, murder. Finally, Jesse saw beyond the deception. His sin began to strike through his heart like a sword. Jesse gave a broken hearted confession, yet he still had to face heart-wrenching consequences for his sins. You see, a baby was born from the adulterous affair, and sadly soon after it was born, it died.

I'm sure by now you have recognized the Biblical story of King David in this retelling. Though this tragic event took place many years ago, the same horrific pattern is carried out time and again every day, all around us, and it all begins with straying feet. Selfish endeavors, time apart from God, ungratefulness, idle thoughts, discontentment, adultery, and death to a home—polluted progressions! Do these evils sound familiar in our society?

Some questions come to mind when considering how people who once walked with God could choose to walk so far away from His will. How did a man after God's own heart end up involved in adultery and murder? Why did Adam and Eve continue to follow Satan's way after tasting the bitter fruit? The answer: guilty feet don't walk with God. They chose to hold to their lust and pride. However, thankfully, when confronted by the Lord, they saw the truth.

The blinders of the enemy were lifted by the Word of God. They suddenly understood that they had terribly strayed. The enemy had deceived them. The enemy had dressed up so many lies, and they had fallen for them. Most horribly, they had grieved the Spirit of God each time He had come to warn them. *"Don't go that way!"* *"Come back!"* *"There is danger!"* *"The path you are walking on leads to death!"*

Read Proverbs 14:12 reads: "There is a way which seemeth right unto a man, but the end thereof are the ways of death."

Let's break this verse down and study it a few words at a time. We will begin with the first two words of Proverbs 14:12. Read the verse and study the first two words.

Which answer below most likely matches the phrase *"There is"*?

a. There possibly is
b. Some say there is
c. Sometimes there is
d. Most certainly there is

Right! The answer is <u>D</u>. When the Bible says *"There is,"* we should certainly conclude that there most certainly is!

Next, we see *"which seemeth right."*

How much trouble would the deceiver go through to make something seem *"right"*? What sin traps of our day seem right?

_____

_____

_____

The snares for man are designed especially to catch a man. We see in the previous verse the phrase, "unto a man". Satan has disguised the path of death to look like the path of life. Many of the things that we watch and listen to each day romanticize sin. Snapshots of glorious sins are flashed before us constantly, desensitizing our soul, distorting truth, and leading us to a deformed desire to want the disgusting and deadly pigpen of this world.

Now, let's take time to complete our review of Proverbs 14:12. We had looked at how man thinks his way is right, but the conclusion of the verse gives us a warning.

"but"

"the end thereof"

"are the ways of death"

What a terrible state it is when we step into the high heels of low living and walk on in our self-chosen path, away from an all-loving Lord. It's a rough and rocky road. It is a dark and lonely way when guilty feet don't walk with God.

# Day Four

# The Cost of Sidestepping God's Command

"For the wages of sin is death;" Romans 6:23

We have seen the need to put away the shoes of the flesh, but we must also consider the cost of Eve's stepping away from God's commands. It is difficult to describe the multitude of sorrows that came from Adam and Eve sidestepping God's command. We looked at the separated walk it caused between God and man, yet where do we begin in sketching out the centuries of death that followed Eden's nightmare? Since we are this close to Eden in our study, let's begin there and contrast the differences between the before and after work of sin. We learned on day one of our study that Eden was without corruption and without harm. All was beautiful and pure. The sidestepping of God's command would demand the cost of all of those pure joys of Eden. Death would permeate every area of life.

Eve chose to step into the flesh, and the shoes of the flesh always lead to death. Sin brings death. Disobedience equals punishment. A price will be paid for wrongdoing. Many people have a tendency to mock the idea of sin and consequence. I've heard things such as:

"I am a good person."

"I may have to pay for it someday, but for now I am going to live it up."

"People have been saying God is coming back soon for years."

We like to hold on to our familiar shoes, don't we? Some people put aside fear if the punishment doesn't quickly follow the crime. However, God promises time after time in the Bible that sin will be dealt with. We can either confess our sin (turn from it, repent), or we reap the full penalty of our disobedience. Looking at Adam and Eve, one might think, wow, they didn't die for a long time after their sin. Please, look a little closer friend. They did die. As soon as they disobeyed God and touched the forbidden fruit, they died. We can see from Genesis 3:3b that God had said *"Ye shall not eat of it neither shall ye touch it lest ye die."* Their spirit within them died immediately upon sinning. They suffered separation from God instantly. Why else would they have been hiding from the God who loved them? At the touch and taste of sin, their souls were slain with death. God had mercy not to allow their bodies to die instantly or, needless to say, man's hope would have been lost forever. Adam's and Eve's bodies saw a slower and progressive form of decay; yet every day they would see the effects of death. Dying cells, weakening bones, aging skin, pain and corruption would be an everyday occurrence for Adam and Eve, as it is still for us today. Consider the tedious work we go through in a day just to cover the look and smell of death in our ever deteriorating bodies. We are constantly doing everything—from brushing decay away from our teeth, to washing and perfuming our bodies continually. The most popular companies among women are those that can exfoliate the dead and make us look a little more alive for a while. Our own bodies testify to the horrid results of sin and the presence of death due to sin. Think about it, reader; there really was a garden. The first man and woman did pass down a sinful nature. We inherited a guilty sentence. Sin is real, and the consequences are as well. We are all born with a sin nature, and sin results in death. All sin has consequences. Consequences of sin may delay, but they will come. God did flood the earth, Sodom and Gomorrah did burn, David did experience tremendous sorrow over his sins of adultery and murder. Sin will revisit us with worse consequence than we ever imagined, unless … we repent. The sins of Adam and Eve were costly. Let's look at some of the consequences that those first sins brought about.

## Untainted Goodness Was Lost

In considering the consequences of Eden, let's first consider the loss of the "goodness" of the earth. Stepping into the shoes of the flesh cost the first man and women goodness. Adam's sin would bring corruption to God's beautiful creation. The ground from which trees and plants grew would become cursed. The earth would become hardened. Sweat and toil would be required for food. Thorns and briars would grow and threaten to choke plants. Death would enfold many plants with disease. Insects and animals would trespass into man's domain and ravish the fruits of his labor. Man's days would be consumed with toil for food. A repetition of hoeing, planting and weeding would constantly precede man's supply of food. Sound familiar? We still suffer the loss of the "goodness" of Eden, don't we? We will until God makes all things new.

## Unguarded Environment Was Lost

Another cost of sin was loss of perfect safety. Friction between man and animals, as well as battles among the animals themselves brought an end to outdoor safety. We know that enmity with the serpent came from Eve's choice to partake of the tree of knowledge of good and evil. It didn't take long for the fruit to produce the knowledge of evil in Eve's mind. The very next time she moved to pet a lion, she knew violence and fear. When Adam made the decision to go for a horseback ride, as my daughter Ashley put it, "being bucked just might have 'thrown' him." Sin had wrought havoc on all of creation. Things that were once in control were violently out of control. By the time that Noah and his family settled on dry land, animals preyed on one another. Upon God's declaration in Gen. 9:2-3 Noah and Mrs. Noah had a sudden need for meat with their potatoes. Sin required a sacrifice—physically, emotionally, and spiritually. The blood of man and woman now needed different elements such as iron and B-12, and animal protein was the main source of what the corrupted blood chemistry required. The animals were no longer safe from man, and man was no longer safe from the animals. The great outdoors wasn't as great as it once had been. Man now needed shelter and protection from the wild beasts as well as dangerous elements of disease and all kinds of danger. A safe dwelling would be needed. The life of an unguarded environment was lost.

## Untouched Purity of Heart Was Lost

Finally, stepping into the shoes of the flesh led to the corruption of the soul. All that God placed in Eden for man to enjoy was "good." God had filled the garden with an abundance of the most amazing pleasures. Prior to sin, everything around Adam and Eve was pure and available for their enjoyment. Every detail of life had been created by God to suit man and woman. Joy was limitless, and there was no space for boredom. All the delights of sky, land, and sea were at man's fingertips. God's fascinating creation waited to reveal new wonders day after day. Man and woman had pure minds and a clear conscience. Even their subconscious thoughts and memories were filled with only pleasant thoughts.

The keenness of their minds must have been amazing as well, seeing that Adam gave all the animals their classified names from an astoundingly sharp wealth of knowledge that was granted him upon his creation. Every neuron, axon and dendrite was working at peek performance. Can you imagine a brain that would put Einstein to shame? In considering the great capacity of the first man's intellect, try to put to mind the thought that all this pure knowledge was focused on worshipping God and caring for one another.

Amazingly, the minds of the first man and woman remained in a constant state of worship. Everywhere the eyes of man looked, they saw God's glory. Any touch of their hands brought fulfillment. Whatever food they tasted was complete with delight and pleasure. Each sound in their ear brought peace and inspiration. The voice of God spoke through the air and was met with the grateful voices of his first son and daughter. Laughter, joy, and thankfulness abounded in Eden's first days. Makes me long for Heaven, how about you?

The love and emotions of man and woman were deep and sincere as well. Each saw to the needs of the other without any hurtful words, walls of defense, or records of wrongs. Their attention and affections were given without bound. Picture it as an ongoing honeymoon. No distractions whatsoever were present to pull their attention away from one another. They worked together and loved together without one single disagreement—until sin. That one thought, touch, and taste of sin would cost them the loss of all the untouched purity of creation.

Take a moment to list some specific details of what Adam and Eve lost:

_____

_____

_____

When we lose something, we grieve. Many times we try to hide and ignore the hurt or fill it with other things. The deeper the loss, the deeper the grief usually is. I know this is a tough question, and I do not want you to write the answer out for this one, but can you relate to Adam and Eve? Do you feel a deep loss caused by sin in your life? Do you feel separated from God? Have you heard His voice asking where you are? He is seeking you. Let us take a moment to ask God to reveal any hidden sin. Ask God to forgive whatever comes to the surface.

Dear Heavenly Father,

Please come now as you did to Adam and Eve and find me too in my garden. I have hidden here for much too long. I miss you, God. I pray that you forgive my sin and restore my walk with you; I long to walk in the freedom of your grace. Thank you for seeking me through your loving convicting power.

In the sweet name of Jesus,
Amen

# Day Five

# Shoes Required

S HOES REQUIRED! Finally, we see the notice in Genesis 3:10-11 that demands the need for the first shoes in the Bible. SHOES REQUIRED! It is in these verses that we see the necessity for the first covering—spiritually, emotionally, and physically. In these verses man is aware of his need for covering. He knows he is undone, and shame rightly follows. Physically, thorns suddenly were underfoot (Gen 3:18), poisons now abounded, serpents could now strike, infection and wounds now loomed, and man and woman were now vulnerable. Emotionally, fear and insecurity now terrorized the mind of man and woman. Spiritually, the worst curse of all had come—a separated walk from God; for as we have seen, guilty feet don't walk with God. God had come (in Genesis 3) to walk with Adam and Eve, yet they, at best, could only hide. God began to question, and they began to excuse. The only treading they did was on each other. Coming to Genesis 3:15, the curse begins, and we see it bringing a bruise to the heel of woman's seed.

What would that bruise mean? It would mean a mortal wound to the Son of man. Two perfect little feet would be born into this world. They would grow and learn to walk. Walking to the poor, blind, lame, lonely and imprisoned—they would bring life. Leaving a perfect and glorious heaven, our sweet Jesus would care more about our desperate, sinful state and unshod feet than the unimaginable pain that would pierce his three-fold person. The perfect feet of Jesus would be nailed to a cross, his soul brutally wounded, His Spirit grieved, and His body scarred. All of this was done so that you and I could once again walk with God. It is the great exchange. Shoes of flesh are surrendered for shoes of grace—dust for divine—amazing love!

Consider the time when the first shoes were required. I imagine Adam and Eve were a terrible sight. They must have looked desperate when God came to them in their hiding spot among the trees. Can't you imagine them pulling and tugging their fig leaves in a frantic attempt to cover themselves? The first man and woman suffered more than they could have imagined in their undone state. Yet, the God of all grace had mercy. In his compassion, He covered them. Not only did their bodies need covering, but their feet also needed a barrier from harm. The first shoes were needed there in Eden to protect the vulnerable feet of man.

Read Genesis 3:21 and write what you observe.

_____

_____

_____

God provided physical coverings from a sacrificed animal. This first sacrifice served as a physical covering as well as pointed to a future spiritual covering in a coming Messiah. The perfect sacrifice of Christ would bruise the head of the serpent and restore a walk with God to all who would accept it.

Many search all of their life to find the coverings that will grant peace and joy. What wonderful news we have. Grace has been provided. The price has been paid for more than a return to Eden. A better than Eden is offered by the precious sacrifice of Jesus. When we accept Jesus as our Lord and ask Him to cleanse our sin, we are given a perfect eternal residency. Eden, as good as it was, held potential sin and death. Heaven will be free of worldly trees of temptation, subtle fleshly snakes, and any influence of Satan, the evil destroyer. Romans 6:23 explains, "For the wages of sin is death; but the gift of God is eternal life through Jesus Christ our Lord." God offers mercy by not giving us what we deserve, and grace by giving us wonderful blessings we don't deserve. He offers with outstretched arms, and with outstretched arms we must receive—totally empty and surrendered. It is only then that we can receive his beautifully perfect covering of grace. The shoes of grace will not only allow man to walk once again with his Creator, God, but our standing in Christ also promises us a permanently secure standing before Him. A perfect home awaits us as well, one perfect and complete, with no threat of corruption or sin. What a standing we have in the shoes of grace.

God offers what many spend their lives trying to gain and buy. He offers grace. Grace is our answer. "God's riches at Christ expense" as we have learned in Sunday School and Church. Grace is the covering that we are searching for, and grace is the covering that will restore our walk with God. As wonderful as Eden was, the grace of God offers something better than Eden. You see, Eden was "very good," but we are now offered perfection. Eden was a pure beginning, yet it was not a complete end until man had been given a choice. Eve chose the tree of knowledge of good and evil, the "high heels" of low living. Accepting Jesus as Savior is our opportunity to partake now of the tree of life and put on the shoes of grace.

In conclusion, Eve had the good life. She had no need to fight mall madness or dress to impress. Nothing was impure or vulnerable in all of her body, soul, or spirit, until she stepped aside. When Eve chose to sin, she stepped out and took her first look at the world, flesh, and the devil. She stooped down to try out the shoes of the flesh. She tried them on for size and at first she was hesitant. They didn't seem to fit! "God hath said ye shall not eat of it, neither shall ye touch it lest ye die," she stated in Genesis 3:3. But the sales pitch continued and Eve would pay dearly for those high heels of low living.

We are not different from Eve; we too wear the shoes of the flesh. One might think that we would welcome the thought of losing these shoes. Yet we insist that these shoes are "broken in." They've been with us so long and we are doing the best we can. So what are we to do? At all cost, we should lose the shoes of the flesh. We can never stand in grace until we are fully broken, and until we have surrendered all that we are standing on.

It has crossed your mind, hasn't it? The shoes of sin are so heavy with all their guilt, disappointments, shame, fear, and lack of joy. They leave us ragged, uncomfortable, unfit, broken, and undone. We are "one-shoers," as was said before, always patching up, hiding, and covering.

Have you been to the Grace Gallery, friend? Have you seen the answer? Many have walked by and seen them (the ruby red slippers of grace). Others have window-shopped, while a few even stopped to try them on. Another group even placed grace on hold, yet no transaction was ever made—no real inquiry. It seemed there was always someone or something to come by and snatch their attention away from the shoes of grace. A cheap "new" covering was thrown in their faces with the line, "Everybody is buying these; they are such a deal." They were labeled *peace*, these cheap imitation coverings, but the real tag read *plague*! The writing-in fine print, of course, read as follows: inner sole made of worldly gain and prosperity. Manmade uppers, lined with self-obtained "religion." Sadly, this tag was not visible, and they passed by the beautiful shoes of grace. Shoes with an eternal life guarantee. *Too expensive*, they thought. Yet, if they would have only looked closer, they would have seen a tag with the inscription—PAID IN FULL BY THE BLOOD OF THE LAMB and signed by Jesus Christ.

Friend, has there been a day in your life when you made an eternal transaction? Have you ever been broken and convicted over your sin to the point that you fully surrendered your life to Christ? If you have, you will remember it; you will have a receipt (a knowledge of that time). When the God of Heaven and earth removes your sin and enters your life, you never get over that. You know that a King has come and his nailed, scarred hands have placed two perfect slippers on your feet. These slippers are labeled "Grace." Are you sure you stand in grace, or are you like a friend of mine, Carolyn Dixon, who bought the cheap imitations. She confessed, *"I began reading the Bible to prove that I was saved, but as I read I found out that I was going to hell."* Carolyn continued, *"I realized that I believed in Jesus like I believed in George Washington."* Jesus was someone she knew about; but Jesus was not someone she knew personally.

Many people will one day cry out to the Lord at his throne. They will attempt to defend their standing; however, unless there has been a day when a transaction was made in their lives, they will face an eternity in Hell. No sinner can stand before a holy God and expect to enter Heaven. No matter how many good things we have done, we are all born into sin, and the blood of Jesus must be applied by way of a broken-hearted prayer of repentance and a humble plea for salvation. Has there been a day when an exchange was made in your life, dear reader? Have you surrendered all that you stand on, to only stand in His Grace? If so, blessed are you—your stand is sure in Christ— and eternal! If not, friend, lose the shoes! You will not be able to stand before almighty God in the high heels of low living. Lose the shoes of sin and flesh. Two nail-scarred feet paid the price so that you can walk with God and forevermore wear His shoes of grace.

If there has never been a time in your life when you have prayed and invited God into your life, I invite you to pray the following prayer.

Dear Lord,

I know that I am a sinner. Believing the promise that you died and rose again to pay for my wrongs, I invite you into my life. Please forgive me. I ask you to come now and be the Lord of my life. I accept your shoes of grace that I may walk forever more with you. Thank you for the promise that you will now never leave me nor forsake me.

In the precious name of Jesus,
Amen

# WEEK TWO

## Shoes of Worship

# Day One

# The Grace to Return

"Come now therefore, and I will send thee unto Pharaoh,
that thou mayest bring forth my people the children of Israel
out of Egypt." Exodus 3:10

While the shoes of grace are a permanent covering for every believer in Christ, there are other shoes that we must daily put on. Genesis pictured Eve putting on the shoes of sinful flesh; Exodus has God instructing Moses to put off the shoes of the flesh when coming into God's presence. We travel now from Genesis 3 to Exodus 3 for our next view of the shoes in scripture. The first shoes of Genesis pointed out the need for a redemptive covering of grace, and the shoes in Exodus follows with a lesson in worship. How fitting this is, for grace should always be followed by worship.

Exodus 3:1 opens with Moses keeping "the flock of Jethro, his father-in-law." Did you catch that, dear reader? Something amazing is about to happen here at an "unamazing" time. During a very routine day, Moses was simply watching the sheep like he had done many times before in an ordinary way at an ordinary time. However, God shows up in the "ordinary" and makes it extraordinary. He transforms daily routine into moments that are eternally significant. Notice, too, that God even takes a seemingly mundane place and restates it as holy ground. This brings us to look, too, at where Moses was during this scene. Moses, the former prince of Egypt, was on the "backside of the desert." In his dictionary, M.C. Easton tells us that "the backside of the desert is west of the desert region, the region 'behind a man,' as the east is the region in front."[1] So we ask, what was behind this man? What regret stood at his back? Previous scripture answers these questions for us.

Beginning in Exodus 2:11, we find Moses, back in Egypt, looking out on his people and seeing their burden. This was when his "backside of the desert" story began. Moses could no longer stand to see his people abused without anyone to stand for them. Secretly watching, he "spied" an Egyptian beating a Hebrew slave. Next, convinced that no one would see him, Moses slew the Egyptian and covered the dead body in the sand. (We will call it the "spy, slay, sand approach.") After two days, Moses came out to see a hot-headed Hebrew smiting his fellow man. Moses questioned him, *"Wherefore smites thou thy fellow?"* (Exodus 2:13 b) The man's response would present a life-shaking blow to Moses—this would surely haunt him in his desert years. *"Who hath made thee prince and a judge over us? Intendest thou to kill me, as thou killest the Egyptian?"* (Exodus 2:14). To Moses' demise, someone had witnessed the murder! This fact is obvious by looking at the second question, yet what was in that first inquiry? ("Who hath made thee prince and a judge over us?") I can't help but wonder if that question resounded time and again in the mind of Moses, Israel's future liberator. Did Satan organize this question, and later use it to have Moses feel unworthy of his call to deliver his people?

"Who are you to lead?" Did the enemy bring this incident to play over and over in the mind of Moses? Did he hammer on Moses' insecurities with every replay of his failure to liberate his people? Did he taunt Moses with: *"You are not able to free anyone; you tried and utterly failed"* so *"Who are you to lead"*? I know he does that to this little lady. Even now as I pen these words, I hear the taunting intimidator of the Christian's soul—*"who are you to write?"* *"Who are you to encourage the women of God?"* Thank God for the true calling that overcomes the schemer's slander. In dealing with this dilemma, I share with you my mother's favorite verse: Philippians 4:13, "I can do all things through Christ that strengthens me."

I am sure you have experienced the battle of worry and worship in your own life. The pull of regret and the desire for rest are constantly at war within us. The answer is worship. Turning aside to God and hearing His Words of guidance will break the chains of regret and open doors of deliverance. Take some time to list some lies used by your enemy. Describe his condemnations and accusations, but don't stop there. Go on to worship God by writing the biblical truths that conquer those lies.

Lies the enemy has used to keep you from God: _____

_____

_____

Biblical promises that dispute these lies: _____

_____

_____

_____

Moses wanted to help his people, but he had attempted to free them in the shoes of the flesh. The flesh frees no man. Moses couldn't set his people at liberty in his own strength, even though he hated their burden; neither can we, friend. God alone can set the captives free, but we cannot in and of our own strength. It must be by His power and His alone. In other words, the "spy, slay, sand approach" didn't work for Moses, and it will not work for you or me. Standing in the shoes of the flesh will not do away with our "Egyptians." We cannot manipulate circumstances to relieve other's oppression. Our people will not be free to go out and worship until we remove our shoes of flesh and meet God on his mountain and worship. It will only be then that we can put on the house-shoes of rest and watch Him deliver.

# Day Two

# The Burning Bush:
# A Call to Step Aside

"And when the Lord saw that he turned aside to see,
God called unto him out of the midst of the bush,
and said, Moses, Moses..." Exodus 3:4

What gets our attention? What draws us away? Is it the wooing of the devil, as with Eve? Or do the wonders of an amazing God call us aside, as with Moses? Is it a new car, a nice home, fame, fortune, a comfortable life, a successful career? Maybe it is our children - maybe we are drawn away to the pursuit of their exaltation in sports, degrees, or titles. It seems most everything draws us away from God's Word and His house. Why are we wooed away as Eve to the apples of achievement? Why do we miss the wonders of God's will? Is it due to fact that we will not step aside in faith to see what God is doing? Maybe it's because there are no bumper stickers that read "My child is an honor student at Backside of the Desert Academy." Even if there were, would we want to display them? What are we pursuing? Does it bring worship to us, or does it bring us to worship God? Worship takes stepping aside, and stepping aside leads to a burning bush.

What does a burning bush look like today? It looks like a time when God speaks to us from His Word. Have you had a burning bush lately? They won't be seen in Egypt. Surprisingly, they are usually found on the backside of the desert—that is where you will see them. They are usually found on the normal days and during broken times. We experience our burning bushes on those days when we are alone with God. It's mostly dry there and few know we are there and even fewer care. We have ended up there because we have been in the desert, as Moses. Most certainly, we are there for God to prepare us for a time of deliverance.

I wonder how often we miss the will of God because we don't "step aside to see" a burning bush. Shepherding on the backside of the desert, Moses saw something that captured his attention. A bush burned, but it was not consumed. Moses was caught away with wonder, and he turned aside to seek the mystery behind this wonder. Now, Moses could have been so downcast with the menial tasks of caring for the flock that he never looked up. No doubt, as was already stated, he had his regrets. The pictures of his suffering brethren more than likely frequented his mind and brought along waves of guilt and remorse. Guilt-remorse, guilt-remorse, like the restless waves of the ocean, they reminded Moses of his desire to set his people free as well as his failed attempt to do so. How encouraging that God was ready to bring Moses to the mountain of God and cover his wounds with worship. Brokenness has always been the path to rest, and so it was with Moses. He had to put himself aside in order to find God's peace and God's purpose, and he did.

I love the text in Exodus 3:4, as it informs us, *"When the Lord saw that he turned aside to see"*—When Moses drew near to God, God called out to Moses. What a wonderful God! What a Redeemer! Knowing that Eve lost her heart for worship by stepping aside to hear the wooing of Satan, we now see that God brings man back to worship by drawing Moses to step aside and see the wonders of God.

"Moses, Moses"—

"Two calls for service," that is how Dr. Fredrick Brabson labels it. In his sermon series entitled "The Urgency of Doubles," Pastor Brabson brings out the personal call of Moses in a dynamic fashion. I give you now his rendition of the call of Moses.

> *"Moses, Moses—Take off thy shoes! You cannot come to God with "all that"—you've got on too much."*
> *"Moses, Moses—There is a powerful individual in Egypt that I am calling you to confront."*
> *"Moses, Moses—There is a tremendous work I am calling you to."* [2]

Dr. Brabson goes on to point out that when a name is called twice, it resounds with a strong urgency. It calls for certain attention, immediate response, and swift obedience. An urgent call is a call filled with strong compassion. Let's take a few moments to reflect throughout scripture and listen in on some calls of the Father, the times when He called names twice. Stop at each and consider the urgency behind it. List the urgency of the mission in the blank beside the call.

II Samuel 18:33

"Absalom, Absalom"—

_____

Luke 10:40-41

"Martha, Martha"—

_____

Matthew 23:37

"Jerusalem, Jerusalem "—

_____

Exodus 3:4

"Moses, Moses"—

_____

I Samuel 3:10-11

"Samuel, Samuel"—

_____

This is what I recorded:

"Absalom, Absalom": <u>a grief stricken cry from a father's heart.</u>

"Martha, Martha": <u>a call to be still and worship.</u>

"Jerusalem, Jerusalem": <u>the Savior's grief over his people denying his comfort</u>

"Moses, Moses": <u>a call to deliver.</u>

"Samuel, Samuel": <u>prepare to be my prophet.</u>

As I write this portion of our study, I am touched with tender emotions remembering a recent experience. A few years ago, I was able to travel to Israel with my mom and dad—what a blessing! As we visited the Sea of Galilee, my heart was especially touched with the thought of Jesus' call to his followers. A threefold question to Peter moved across the waves of time to prick my own heart. "Lovest thou me? Feed my lambs." "Lovest thou me? Feed my lambs." "Lovest thou me? Feed my sheep." (John 21:13-17)

I have felt a strong calling to teach women of God to study the Bible fervently. This strong call now moved to urgent with my own shore side experience. My mom and dad were making their way back to the tour bus. It was time to go, but I lingered. I wanted to take in all I could before going. That's when Dad called my name (twice), "*Patty ... Patty.*" "*Coming!*" I replied to my earthly dad, and,

*"Here I am,"* I answered to my Heavenly Father. Take a minute yourself. Think back on your own youthful years, reader. Do you remember the times your parents or a loved one called your name? How about the times that your Heavenly father called you to a certain service? If you have never experienced God's commissioning call, I pray you will soon hear his voice ring out to you. God is calling you to rest, preparation, and worship, but you must first put aside the shoes of worry. Place your names in the blanks below. Notice what the voice of God is calling you to.

_____, _____ Come and rest.

_____, _____ Come and prepare.

_____, _____ Come and worship.

Many run from the call of God. Fear of the unknown drives them to shrink back. Now the next time you hear your call, simply respond, *"Hear I am!"*

Isaiah spoke it: *"Here am I send me"* (Isaiah 6:8)

Mary humbly responded (Luke 1:38), *"Behold the handmaid of the Lord; be it unto me according to thy word."*

Samuel voiced it, *"Speak; for thy servant heareth."* (I Samuel 3:10)

Paul confessed, *"Who art thou, Lord?"* (Acts 9:5)

John *"I fell at his feet as dead"* (Rev. 1:17), and

Jesus responded, *"I lay down my life"* (John 10:18).

They all responded to the call of the urgent mission. How about your Heavenly call? If you don't know your spiritual call to a purpose God has just for you—ask him, listen closely, watch for the "burning bush" in your everyday routine, and by all means, friend, step aside.

# Day Three

# Take Off Your Shoes:
# A Call to Lay Aside Shoes of Worry for Shoes of Worship

After Moses pleased God in stepping aside to see the burning bush, God then required him to lay aside his shoes of insecurity. The call to *"put off thy shoes from off thy feet"* is a call to put off the flesh and to put on spiritual shoes of worship. God reveals His ways to those who will step aside to seek him and lay aside fleshly weakness to obey him. Consider the minds of godly men and women in God's word who stepped aside to follow and laid aside all they were standing on to worship God. What did they lay aside?

Consider the many examples in scripture of godly men and women who removed the shoes of the flesh to worship God. I have written the verses that show their surrender. For those of you who would like further study, search out the scriptures that show the other side of their surrender and obedience—their blessing. I have marked some possible places with an asterisk * to help you find these. Write out what you learn from their obedience. Enjoy!

Noah laid down his life agenda to follow God's plan and to save a remnant. He was willing to follow God by faith even through the wilderness. Genesis 7:5

*See Hebrews 11:7 _____ .

Abraham offered his only son, willing to sacrifice the evidence of God's promise in order to fully worship God in full obedience. The Lord, in return, rewarded Abraham exceedingly. Genesis 22:3-5

* Genesis 22:16-18 and Hebrews 11:8-10 _____

_____

Joseph pushed away the temptation of fleshly lust in order to honor God; he was blessed with position and purpose. Genesis 39:12

*Genesis 41:39 _____

Moses refused to be called a son of a Pharaoh and obeyed God in leading His people to freedom. Hebrews 11:24-29

*Hebrews 11:24-29 (Both surrender and reward can be found in the Hebrews passage.)

_____

_____

We can see in the life of Ruth a putting behind of country and homeland in order to follow God in blind faith. Ruth was then placed in the family as one who would have a part in the lineage of Christ. Ruth1:16

*See Matthew 1:5. _____

Job sat down away from his riches to seek God (Job 13:15). Job even prayed for his friends (Job 42:10). God gave him patience as well as multiplied blessings.

*Job 42:10-17 _____

Others such as Daniel neither bowed to the king's idols nor ate of his bounties and therefore gained a pure vision of God. Daniel 1:8

*See Daniel 7:9_____

Many others in the Bible put off their agendas to come before God and receive His restful shoes of worship.

In the New Testament, Mary, the mother of Christ, sweetly accepted God's unusual plan. She abandoned her own ideas to secure the peace of trusting God's ways. Luke 1:38

*The blessing can also be found in Luke 1:38 _____ .

John, the revelator, suffered the trials of exile to exalt The Lamb of God and was given a vision of the very throne room of Heaven. Revelation 1:9

* See Revelation 1:17-20 _____

Then there was Mary Magdalene who cast away the scarlet coverings of lust to gain a sacrificial heart of worship. Luke 8:1-2

* See Mark 16:9

The apostle Peter put off his desire for men's approval to live a sacrificial life of service; he was given a steadfast mind like a rock—sure and sturdy. Acts 3:12

* See Acts 4:13-14 _____

Finally, our Jesus sacrificed his life from the cradle to the cross, in order to give us life everlasting, and now he forever reigns as our Lamb. John 19:30

*See Luke 1:33 _____

Each of these chose to surrender the bindings of the flesh for shoes of worship. While standing before God in pure worship, they discovered His plan and purposes.

These obedient ones chose to lay aside the worldly shoes of insecurity for shoes of worship. Contemplate the lives that we have mentioned. These spiritual victors were moved from the binding of fleshly temptations to the freedom of walking in the Spirit of God. Fill in the areas below, telling what you remember about each one who laid aside something to worship God and respond to his call.

|  | *What they put aside: | *What they put on: |
|---|---|---|
| Noah | _____ | _____ |
| Abraham | _____ | _____ |
| Joseph | _____ | _____ |
| Moses | _____ | _____ |
| Ruth | _____ | _____ |
| Job | _____ | _____ |
| Daniel | _____ | _____ |
| Mary | _____ | _____ |
| Paul | _____ | _____ |
| Mary Magdalene | _____ | _____ |
| Jesus | _____ | _____ |

* If you have difficulty, just move on to the end of today's study for the completed chart.

The call to *"put off thy shoes"* is a serious imperative. We must obey this instruction still today if we are going to ever hear from a holy God. As Moses literally removed his shoes to approach God, we must spiritually "put off" any worldliness before coming before our great King. Anything we are standing on apart from God's word must be placed aside. Then, and only then, can we come to God and worship. We must "put off" our shoes of worldliness in order to worship.

The practice of removing shoes before entering a place of worship has long been practiced in the Middle East. We know of many families who have an unspoken rule of "shoe off at the door please." It's not hard to figure out when you have entered one of these homes. There is usually a neat row of shoes just inside the threshold. There may even be a nicely placed rug placed by the door for a helpful clue. In kindness, the hostess assures you there is no need to remove your shoes, however in reality she would prefer it. God didn't leave Moses guessing. He gave him no option. God's expectation was plain and clear *"PUT OFF THY SHOES."* Moses obeyed God and removed what he was standing on. He "put away" his shoes. The shoes represented uncleanness (contact with the world). God revealed His ways to Moses only after Moses had stepped away from his own understanding. Still today, God reveals his will to those who are willing to walk away from the foundations they have trusted and come before God without any other soul dependency.

Sadly, many miss true worship and consequently don't know God's ways. Why is this? They don't remove their "shoes". My husband recently shared an example of this with me. A young man met with him and proceeded to share about his desire to go into an area of ministry. This fellow wanted to begin preparing for leadership. He was ready to jump into ministry, but he had never "put off" his shoes of worldliness. His story was that he thought he was ready to lead others, yet he, himself, had never surrender his all to the leadership of God.

There were things he had not set aside. Shoes of the world were still clinging to his feet as he approached the mountain of God's call. His thoughts were that he was ready to train for the ministry. The facts were he had several vices and addictions that he had not stepped aside from. God's call to "put off" our shoes is a very serious one. No drowning person can help another who is struggling to stay above water. Church leaders, church workers, Sunday school teachers, youth leaders and pastors are to be surrendered and proven. Those fresh out of Egypt need time for their desert disciplines and trainings before standing to lead others to freedom. Seminary and Bible colleges are not hospitals; they are spiritual boot camps and military post. The church is to be the place for the spiritually wounded and a place where they can be made whole. It should be the place where spiritual infants grow and receive good nourishment. Leadership takes time. It's not something man chooses, but it is something God decides.

Only as we mature in Christ will we be ready to put off the selfish and worldly standings and lead others to the Promised Land. When we fully surrender our plans, we can come and hear God's agenda of how to free his people. We must take off our shoes in exchange for a new pair of shoes that will allow us to tread over difficult circumstances and carry out God's work. These shoes will be just what we need to do the spiritual task that God calls us to. You see, for every shoe that we put off, God gives spiritual shoes to put on.

To find God's purpose, we must put on his house shoes of rest and worship. Relaxing in his promises to perform the work he began, we can walk on in his special coverings. These shoes will allow us to rest in the midst of sorrow and trouble, for we can now stand as Moses on God's "I am."

*Completed chart:

| | Put aside: | Put on: |
|---|---|---|
| Noah | his life agenda | Kingdom Work |
| Abraham | his only son | faith |
| Joseph | temptation | self-control |
| Moses | ruling in Egypt | obedience |
| Ruth | her future | submission |
| Job | comfort and honor | patience |
| Daniel | King's food /ease | fasting and prayer |
| Mary | her reputation and fears | peace |
| Paul | prestige | praise |
| Mary Magdalene | attention of men | worship |
| Jesus | His life | service |

# Day Four

# His "I AM" for My "I Am Not"

## "I Am That I Am" Exodus 3:14

In Exodus 3:6, we see God use the word "*moreover*." This word, "moreover", gives the idea "in addition to." God had just informed Moses that he, Moses, was standing on holy ground. As we have witnessed in scripture, holy ground is very sacred. It is to be respected and the one who makes it holy is to be revered. Holy ground to Jewish believers was an area that had been set apart or sanctified. God's presence had met with man there, and God had revealed himself in a special way on that ground. In the Bible, we read that certain places are holy because God has written his name in those areas, such as Israel and Jerusalem. In other words, God's Word is there, and knowing that His word lives, His presence abides there still. It is Holy ground. An imprint of his presence abides there.

We have all seen footprints and handprints of famous people. Movie stars, singers, athletes and such have all left their marks on tourist attractions. People come from far and wide to see these attractions. With cameras in hand, they want to have their picture made at these memorial sites. How much more are we to honor a perfect and holy God? At Mt. Horeb, God's presence stood before Moses, then God revealed to Moses who He was. Now note, anytime this occurs in scripture, the next human response is a "woe is me" experience. "Who am I!" is the humble question from the unworthy observer. We have already looked at the "Woe is Me" responses in scripture and we will look at this honest confession of "Who am I" more later on, yet first let us go according to the text order and look first at God's identity of *"I am that I am."*

God had just made something clear to Moses in Chapter 3 of Exodus. There God told Moses of His holiness. Every act of worship begins with the realization that Almighty God is Holy, and that mankind is not. We cannot stand before him in our pride, self-righteousness, self-pity or worldly pursuits and secret sins—all the "stuff" we chase after must be put off. In Psalms 24:3-4, the author asks, "Who shall ascend into the hill of the Lord or who will stand in his holy place?" then he answers with, "He that hath clean hands, and a pure heart; who hath not lifted up his soul unto vanity, nor sworn deceitfully." God is holy, and we are not. In addition to His declaration of holiness, God states his record of faithfulness to Moses. "Moreover he said, I am the God of thy father, the God of Abraham, the God of Isaac, and the God of Jacob"(Exodus 3:6). Let's break this down and study each phrase.

God was revealing to Moses how he had watched over him. The great "I am" was continuing the covenant now to Moses that had begun long ago. First of all, God's revelation as, *"The God of thy father"* told Moses that God had been the one who watched over

Moses' father. Secondly, *"The God of Abraham,"* revealed God as provider to Moses' forefather. In Abraham's most crucial test, God provided a ram. *Jehovah Jireh, "God the provider",* would now be there to provide for Moses as well. Next, we read of God proclaiming to Moses that He was the *"God of Isaac."* To Isaac God allowed Himself to be known as *Adonai, Avinu* or *"God our Father."* Through Isaac's life, God proved to be a faithful father who asked for hard and unordinary sacrifices, but yet could always be trusted. Finally, the God of Jacob—*Adonai, Eloheikhem* would bring a personal bridge as *"The Lord your God."* [3]

Do we take time to consider the God we stand before? God is the Almighty author who is continuing our life story through a plan He began long ago. We stand before the great "I Am." Yet do we acknowledge his grand presence? In Exodus 3:6(b), the word of God says that *"Moses hid his face"* upon standing in God's presence. He was afraid to look upon God. Moses realized this was the Almighty Jehovah God who had been with his father and forefathers before him. We touched earlier on those in the Bible who saw God then responded, "Who am I." Others confessed "Woe is me." Now it was Moses' turn to experience the awe of God.

Take a moment to record special times of worship you have experienced.

---

---

What made that time special?

_____

_____

When we really step aside to come before God's presence, we find we are undone before a most perfect and holy God. Every man or woman's salvation begins there. Each person desiring salvation must broken-heartedly confess, *"Lord, I am a sinner, please cleanse my sin and be my Lord."* In other words, we must admit our "I am not" and accept His "I am." Moses confessed *"Who am I."* Mary called herself a maidservant of the Lord, John fell as a dead man, and Paul asked, *"Who art thou, Lord?"*

I remember once, during my college years, having a "woe is me" and "who am I" kind of day. During a very discouraging season, I listed to God all of my "I am nots." I poured out my heart with pitiful ramblings such as: "Lord, I am not good at…, I have failed in…, and I feel that I am half doing…." After my confessions, the Lord met me at all my "I am nots" and answered, "No, you are not," but "I Am" and all my "I Ams" are in you as I—your God—am with you. Lovingly, He assured me of the point that it is not about who I was not. When he saved me, it became—and still forever will be—who He is! It was one of those WOW moments of revelation. I went from the pits to praise. It is His "I am" that matters! It is who He is, and not who we are not.

Would you take a moment to list and pray for others you know who are struggling with who they are not over who Jesus is?

_____

My favorite Bible verse, Philippians 1:6, reminds me that my life is part of God's continuing work.

Take a moment to look up this verse and fill in the blanks.

"Being _____ of this very thing, that ____which hath _____ a good work in you will _____ it until the day of Jesus Christ." We can put on the shoes of worship, friends, and rest in His "I Am."

It is God's "I Am" that matters. Interestingly, if you read the scriptural account, God had given Moses the answer "I Am" before Moses had asked the question "Who am I?" yet like myself, Moses missed it. The answer is the "I Am of God" (who God is), not who we are not. God had first addressed this issue of worship with Moses, but Moses, as we, quickly put it aside to the point that it angered God. Moses stayed too long in his "I am nots" and didn't stay in God's "I am," yet God moved him to hold fast only to the mighty hand of an almighty God to deliver Moses and his people.

How are you doing with those "woe is me" times or those "I am nots"? If you have had some of those lately, come now and step into the house shoes of worship. Focus only on His "I am." True worship humbles us: it shows us who we are not and who God is. We must confess our wrongs, yet not hang out in the gutter of our woes. Instead, God calls us to move on from the pits to praise, and all the while exalt His worthiness and ability to perform what he calls us to do.

# Day Five

# A Call to Reserve

F inally, the call to worship is a call to reserve. We gather all God's heavenly words of instruction from the mountain of worship and we secure them for later use in addressing the "elders of Israel" as we carry out our call. We will surely need them as well, for our "Pharaohs."

Take some time to read Exodus 3:7-22, and Exodus 4:1-9.

What information was God giving Moses to store up for his later work in Egypt?

_____

_____

What divine attributes of God's nature did God want Moses to focus on?

_____

What instructions did God give to Moses in the third chapter of Exodus?

_____

_____

We must cherish God's instructions and make sure we give earnest heed to all He says. We will need it later. We must secure His words as Mary, the mother of Jesus did. Luke 2:19 records, "But Mary kept all these things and pondered them in her heart." Surely, the words she reserved from the angel of the Lord, as well as the words from Simeon and Anna, comforted her as she endured trials that passed through her soul like swords. What ponderings do you have, friend? Have you recorded and reserved the words God has spoken to you on your mountaintop of worship? You will need them for the tasks he is sending you to fulfill.

The first truth Moses was to reserve in his heart was that the Great "I Am" had appeared to him. God reviewed his promises to the patriarchs of old—Abraham, Jacob, and Isaac (Ex 3:6).

What have you learned about why God made mention of these past patriarchs?

_____

_____

For sure and certain, God is a God who keeps His Word and holds to His covenant through generations. Have you ever considered the prayers that were made for you by your mother, father, grandparents, family, neighbors, and friends? No man lives to himself. Moses was a part of a bigger work than he ever realized. The Faithful covenant keeper was continuing a great work that He had started years ago in Moses' ancestors. God's plans for you are good. He loved you long before you were ever thought of, and He will continue that which He has started.

The next declaration was that God sees the pain of his people. *"I have surely **seen** the affliction of my people,"* said the Lord. He continues, *"I have **heard** their cry by reason of their taskmasters."* Then it goes even deeper: *"I **know** their sorrows."* Oh, the love of God! He weeps with us in our agony. He keeps our tears in a bottle as the Psalmist mentioned in Ps. 56:8. He knows our pain and he is working to redeem every detail of our sorrow.

Whatever God is leading you to, remember it all begins with turning aside, and turning aside only comes from focusing your full attention on God. Be assured there is a personal call for you. With urgency he speaks your name, and twice he calls it. The call is important. His people are in bondage. Will you come? Don't miss your burning bush. You may see it today! He can catch you away with wonder just as he did with Moses, on an ordinary day, and when He does— Lay aside worry. Come and worship.

*"Take off your shoes, Moses, you are on holy ground,"* God commanded. As Moses approached his burning bush, he was told to remove his shoes. I believe Moses had to be obedient to the first instruction before he could continue to encounter God. May we, as Moses, put off the shoes of daily cares, taking all the problems and pressures of life, and put them aside. Then we can come just as we are.

There, in His presence, we will be comforted. We will see through pure eyes. We will see God! We will hear Heaven's voice call. Heaven's touch will be felt as we sense God near. Then, we will be more than ready to depart and continue our work as we stand in Heaven's covering. We will carry with us his words and his majesty. The appearance of God will be high and lifted up in our mind's eye. A continuance of falling before his throne and at his feet will consume our lives and we will walk in worship. In closing, as we go forth, we will be compelled to obey, for we know He is worthy. We will go with His glow upon us for we will descend from his holy mountain in shoes of worship.

Have you ever had God call you to carry out a certain task for Him? God not only calls, but He also equips the called. What spiritual group do you feel called to minister to?

_____

_____

Share this calling with a mentor and trusted friend, and ask them to join you in prayer over this call.

Take some time on the mountain of worship today to listen to God's divine instructions. You will need them later in your travels to your "Egypt" as you take your message of deliverance to a hurting people.

As we finish this chapter, take some thought on the change Moses experienced in one ordinary day.

What was Moses doing when he saw the bush? _____

What caught his attention about this bush? _____

How long do you think God had been planning to use Moses as Israel's deliverer?

_____

What can the story of Moses teach you in your walk with God?

_____

Good Job! I know you have reserved treasures this week. Hold on to these truths, you will need them later in your calling.

Well, we have covered a lot of ground this week, dear reader, and desert ground at that. First, we saw that God will find us even if we are on the "backside of the desert," and by His grace He will redeem our regrets. Secondly, God gives us a wonderful calling that is personal and specific to the task He wishes us to fulfill. Thirdly, in order to carry out this work, we must exchange our worry for worship. Next, we were encouraged that it is His "I AM" and not our "I am not" that will carry us through. Finally, God gives us the message that we are to reserve until the day of declaration. It has been a wonderful time on the mountain of worship. I pray God will bless you richly as you exchange worry for worship and go down from your mountain to serve in the shoes of worship. You will need to keep these shoes near for your next journey. It is from this mountain that we descend and obtain another pair of shoes—the shoes of warfare.

# WEEK THREE

## Shoes of Warfare

# Day One

## Off with Shoes of Self-Reliance and On with Shoes of Warfare

"And the captain of the Lord's host said unto Joshua, Loose thy shoe from off thy foot; for the place whereon thou standest is holy. And Joshua did so." Joshua 5:15

Our third look at shoes in the Bible takes us to the book of Joshua, where we will learn that Joshua will be asked to hand over some shoes as well. What shoes must this fine warrior cast aside? He will have to remove the military boots of self-reliance. These carnal combat boots must be removed from Israel's new leader so that he, in turn, could put on God's shoes of warfare.

Moses had led the Israelites out of Egypt, and now Joshua would lead them into the Promised Land. To enter into this mighty, inhabited land and tread over the great stronghold of Jericho would require nothing less than God's plan of battle. Joshua could not march in with his own plan of attack, and something deep within him knew that. More than likely, that's why we see him taking a late night, soul-searching stroll that would end up near Jericho. It was then that Joshua was met by the captain of the Lord's host. The commanding warrior ordered Joshua to "loose his shoe" from off his foot, declaring that the place where he stood was holy ground. There, in the shadow of the enemy's camp, Joshua would receive God's counsel for war. A great angel-warrior from heaven had come with a supernatural plan of attack. Through this messenger, God met Joshua and told him he was well able to overtake Jericho, yet it would only come by God's strength and God's battle plan.

As Moses, Joshua would come to learn that one must seek God in every matter of life, especially in leadership. Sounds great, right? However, we see that the plans that God gave Joshua, just like the ones he gives to us, don't fit the bill of human normality. Dr. Fredrick Brabson gives a humorous picture of God's instructions to Moses in freeing the Egyptians. He says *"Now, if we were Moses, we may have thought,* Okay, okay, I got it, God. The reason you want to use me is because of my military experience."* Now, look at Pastor Brabson's idea of God's response to Moses, *"No, no, no, we are going to go with flies, knats, and locusts."* [1]

As we can observe in the battles of the Bible, our heavenly commander has very different plans from the plans that we have. For a certainty, God's ways are wise, but to the world they seem foolish. I Cor.1:27 informs us that He "confounds" the wisdom of the wise. No one can understand God's plans apart from faith. Revelation comes by the Spirit of God imparting His ways to man. As hard as we may try, we cannot figure Him out. Surely, Joshua had many tactics and ideas going over in his mind, but I kind of doubt any one of those included marching quietly, shouting wildly, and blowing horns without any attempt to charge the city. Let us take a note then. Jericho was the first bold barrier in the claiming of the Promised Land, right? What lesson can we learn here? First, we can learn a simple lesson: The first step in conquering a stronghold of Satan is to lose the shoes of self-planning and seek God's shoes of warfare in asking His plan of battle.

My husband often tells me, "Sweetheart, You have it made. All you have to do is listen to me. As your leader, I will tell you what to do and what is best." Of course, you know, dear reader, that I always do just that. With cheerful submission, I wake every day to do everything that I should do. (Don't pass out yet, I was just joking) I wish I could say that were true, but, to be honest, I struggle daily to keep from my own ways. I even sometimes forget to ask God his plans for my daily battles. However, when I do submit to my leaders, it all goes amazingly better, with my dear husband and with God.

The call for Joshua to lose the shoes of self-reliance was not an easy command. Yet, obeying a hard order from higher rank is something every good soldier accepts. He knows every order must be carried out, immediately and without question. The call to untie our thoughts and surrender our battle plans to our angel of the Lord's host is not an easy one, since we like to be in charge. However, we should pause to remember Jesus is the only one who can defeat Satan. We must wear His shoes to tread over the old serpent, the devil. Then we can hold to the promise that we can be "more than conquerors" through Christ (Rom. 8:37).

You can tell a lot about people from their shoes. For the angel of the Lord's host to command Joshua to "loose" his shoes would imply that his shoes were well bound around his feet. That was respectable, was it not? Just like a good young soldier in our day, one of the first rules ingrained in boot camp is the one that everything must be in order. Since a soldier must always be prepared, new soldiers are drilled daily to make sure everything is secure and up to standard, even an unfastened boot could be of critical importance during combat. Everything counts. Being unshod could be costly. Having one's shoes unbound could cost them and others their very lives.

Take a moment to read I Corinthians 14:40.

According to this verse, what things should we have in order?

_____

_____

Did you note the word "all"? Wow, apart from jumping to our fleshly obsessive-compulsive tendencies, how do we ever accomplish doing *all* things "decently and in order" (especially when we don't even know the order)? The truth is, just as Joshua, we have no idea what order to follow. God's guidance is of utmost importance in our daily pursuits, and especially in warfare. As Joshua, we must take time daily to seek God's plans and be willing to relinquish our own ideas— no matter how different His Jericho plans may be.

We must note, too, that even though Joshua was a trained warrior, he must have had areas of insecurity. How do we know this? We see God reassure him. Time and again, the Lord tells Joshua to be strong and very courageous. Maybe the struggle came from the loss of Moses, his leader. Maybe disheartened memories haunted him. After all, he and Caleb had wanted to go up and conquer the area earlier, but no one wanted to follow their walk of faith. All others thought it sounded impossible. Since no one followed his zealous ideas when they first entered Canaan, would they now? Whatever the circumstances Joshua faced, it had to be an adjustment to arise and be the man in charge. It also had to be difficult to trust God, an unseen leader over military experience. We have little problem believing our way is best. Every warrior struggles with the pull of trusting his own thoughts verses trusting God's ways.

The enemy of our souls has a way of whispering convincing plans into our minds as well. When the enemy comes to entice us to some good plan with great tactics and well-marked maps, we dare not trust his allurements. We must be as Abraham and not even take a shoe latchet from a vain king, and especially not from Satan's bidding to make us rich (Genesis 14:23). So we see that not only are we to put away our own self-reliance, we are also to cast aside the enemy's alternatives (II Corinthians 10:5-6). To do this, we need God's discernment. We need our heavenly commander to shed light on the enemy's schemes. We also need to recognize vain pursuits, such as money, success, or fame that only lead to further insecurities when they are pursued without God. With God's commissioning, we are to put aside the shoes of self-reliance.

In conclusion, we realize that even Joshua, a great man of valor, had to be instructed to remove anything he was trusting on in himself to bring victory. No "make it happen" mentality could do it for him. "Pulling himself up by his own boot straps" wouldn't bring down Jericho; it would only have brought down Joshua. Joshua would need something much more powerful. He would have to be shod with the gospel shoes of peace. Ephesians 6:15 instructs us to have our feet shod with "the preparation of the gospel of peace." What does that mean exactly? It means having our minds absolutely assured. It means that we focus on **relaying** the gospel message of peace over **reacting** in our insecure flesh. In making an advance toward a stronghold, we must know that we belong to Christ. We must possess the confidence that He will take care of whatever comes to us. In this mindset, we can have perfect peace. Peace with God, peace with ourselves, and peace to offer every man. Not only are we secure in this peace, we are well prepared to share the gospel of Christ every day, and we are prepared to advance in spiritual battle in God's shoes of warfare.

# Day Two

## The Goods Go to God
## Not Even a Shoe Latchet

As Joshua, we are to remember—the spoils of Jericho go to God. The victory is for His glory. As we learned yesterday we can take a lesson from Abraham and not even take a shoe latchet from a vain king, (Genesis 14:23). The first bounty of Israel's victory in the promised land was to go to God.

Just as the first of all our increases goes to God, threshold offerings go to Him as well. It never pays for us to think we can keep the bounty of our Jerichos. It only cost—greatly. I'm sure ancient forensics could attest to that. If the ashes of Achan could speak, we would hear a lesson in how much it cost to keep the spoils that are to go to God. In Joshua 7, we read about the terrible account of—as I like to put it –*Achan aching in Achor*. Achan, his family, and his animals were stoned and then burned. Why? You may ask why a man was treated so harshly just after winning the stronghold of Jericho. Note that the main lesson of Jericho was to depend on God as they entered the promise land. The goods were to go to God in a way of saying, "You brought us here God—You won the battle, and we give you the total sum of this first offering to show our faith in you to lead us still."

What had Achan done? In the prior chapter, Joshua strongly commanded that no one was to take anything from this battle. It was the first, and it was to go to God (Joshua 6:17-19). Details were even spelled out. No silver, no gold, no brass, and no iron were to be taken, and whoever did take it would be accursed.

Take some time to read Malachi 3:10-11. We normally read verse 10 and stop short of verse 11. God's people are told in verse ten to bring the tithe to the storehouse. This is the first portion (at least a tenth) of our gross income plus our offerings. Offerings are what we want to give above the tithe amount from an overflowing heart of thanks. However, the next verse goes on to warn us that failing to honor God with the first of all our increases leaves us open to the enemy's devouring of all we have! Have you ever thought of the giving of your tithes as a part of your spiritual warfare? Think about it. What are we doing when we obey the command to give God His portion first? We are putting our faith in action. We are laying before his feet the first and asking Him to bless it as well as the remaining. Not only are we saying we trust God, we are also *showing* we trust God. This is done by giving up the first part of all we receive. Does God need our money? No, but we need the constant practice of faith in form of application. Just as Achan, if we try to keep what belongs to God, we will lose what we do have. Our "goods" will be left vulnerable and unprotected—cursed. We often hear of people coming in to a wealth of money, only to waste it away a short time later. Gains that are not blessed under God become losses, and when we try to hold that which God gave to begin with, we could lose all.

Why was Achan's sin so wrong? _____

_____

How did this one man's sin affect all Israel? _____

_____

What things in particular had Achan taken? Circle one.

A. Golden cups

B. Rubies

C. Expensive spices

D. Silver, a wedge of gold, and a Babylonish garment

The correct answer of course is <u>D</u>. Upon seeing these items, Achan confessed that he coveted them (Joshua 7:21). He probably made a mental list of what all he was going to buy with these fine goods in the Promised Land. (Once things settled down and everybody forgot about the command.) Why, he may have even justified his conscience by promising part of it to the tabernacle, but that never happened. Instead, all was lost. It definitely wasn't worth it for Achan to rely on self, was it? It is not for us either, friend.

I know it is difficult to obey the command to tithe when your bills will not add up on paper. Faith never adds up on paper. However, let me be one to testify that obeying God brings blessing, and seeing God provide for our needs in ways we can't imagine, in turn, builds faith. I have seen my husband many a time try to subtract our needs from our income. It doesn't add up on paper because we cannot calculate God. His ways of provision are above our ways. More than likely, it wouldn't be our choice to meet our needs by asking a widow lady to bake us a cake with her last bit of flour and oil as God had Elijah to do. Nor, in turn, would it be like us to be as the widow lady and believe the giving of our last meal to a stranger would be God's means of abundance. God's way is different from ours. It doesn't include holding on to what we have fought for; instead, it requires giving what has been won in our greatest battles over to Him. By the way, wasn't it His plan that took Jericho to begin with?

It takes the Lord to define our Jerichos. I had one not long ago. The Lord revealed it as a Jericho from the beginning. Leading up to one of my conferences, the spiritual warfare had been tremendous, from without and within. I knew God was going to bring down walls, but let me tell you, it took His plan of battle to do it. He led me circle by circle around my Jericho, and when the battle was over, I knew all the goods were to go to God. It was a "stepping over the threshold of home" time. It wouldn't make sense to the world to not keep the best spoils, but it makes sense when you want to please a loving God. May God bless the doorpost of your promise land, reader, as you offer returned thanks for your Jericho by giving all the goods back to God.

Dig Deeper: (Optional work)

Take some time to read on in the book of Joshua. List some distinctions contrasting the Battle of Jericho to the other battles that Joshua would encounter.

_____

_____

How was Jericho different? _____

_____

Why do you think they could keep all the spoils from other battles, yet not Jericho?

_____

_____

_____

# Day Three

# Shaking Out Scorpions

Amazingly, God's peace strengthens us and helps us to tread over scorpions in order to deliver the oppressed. As the warriors of Israel camped nightly in the desert, they had to shake out their boots on occasions. Scorpions and other deadly creatures like to hide out in dark, cool places. Just like the desert warriors of old, we must shake out our boots of peace. You see, there may be a scorpion looming there, in the dark recesses of our combat boots. Scorpions are dreadfully painful. We dare not neglect to check for them in our desert wars.

What might your scorpion be? Does fear, guilt, lying, doubt, or greed loom in the dark recesses of your peace? Does some dark, striking emotion sneak into your life over and over? Friend, shake your boots out! There is a serpent that wants to strike your heel. Heed to the promise that Jesus has crushed his head, and shake off this terror. Shake off the pattern of this world; scorpions can be deadly (Deuteronomy 8:15), their sting is tragic. However, God's word promises us in Luke 10:19, "Behold I give unto you power to tread on scorpions, and over all the power of the enemy: and nothing shall by any means hurt you." Does anyone besides me feel like you have scorpions looming in your boots? Take heart, friend; there is hope.

Realize the power of God's shoes of warfare. They are shoes of iron and brass as we are told in Deuteronomy 33:25, "Thy shoes shall be iron and brass; and as thy days, so shall thy strength be." The soles of ancient shoes were sometimes plated with iron and brass. Some had the enemies' symbol or image engraved on the bottom of their shoes. I love the prophecy of Malachi 4:3, "And ye shall tread down the wicked; for they shall be ashes under the soles of your feet." We need not fear, friend, but instead, as Joshua, we are to be shod (ready) with the gospel of peace and not the flesh. Only the full atonement of Christ can keep us standing in battle. "At-one-ment," that's how Rev. William Boyd Bingham breaks it down. Peace brings us close (at-one) with Christ, knowing we are: justified, redeemed, reconciled, and purged. Take some time to look up the definitions for the following words. Record your definitions in the blanks provided.

Justified- _____

_____

Redeemed- _____

_____

Reconciled-_____

_____

Purged- _____

_____

Can you think of some other Biblical terms that describe our "at-one-ness" with God? If so, list them:

_____

_____

_____

Hopefully, these words gave you the realization that you are set apart and cleansed. As a Christian—you are! In Christ you are seen as holy and "at one" with God. Many times, our spiritual walk is threatened by the scorpions of shame and accusation. Satan gladly accuses us of guilt. He attempts to crawl in our boots and cover us with paralyzing shame and pain. Pick up the Word of God and allow it to shake out those poisonous lies. Knowing truths from God's Word does some shaking! The wonderful promise of John 8:32 encourages us to realize that truth will "make" us free. God's truth has power; we need to keep it in our hearts and minds so it can shake the scorpions from our boots.

Not only do the scorpions of shame make us feel separated, another familiar danger frequently tries to invade our boots of warfare. That intruder is none other than the poisonous scorpion of doubt. Moses was no stranger to this danger that threatened his walk with God. Joshua, too, had to shake out this unwanted pest. God's soldier cannot walk with doubt in his shoe, it will take him down. How then do we deal with this desert danger, you ask. First of all, we must make it a daily practice upon arising to shake out our boots of warfare, ridding any thoughts of doubt that may have crept in. The *what-ifs* and the *hows* have to go. Secondly, we must courageously strap on our boots of peace knowing God will make a way, and He will bring victory as we obey his plan of battle by faith. I would like to share a reading with you now that kind of puts it all into perspective. My husband has had it in his sermon/ illustration collection for years and I am not sure where he found it, but I'm sure you will enjoy this short piece on faith.

## RATIONALIZATION

### The Faith Extinguisher

*What would have happened had Moses tried to figure out all that was needed to accomplish God's command?*

*One of the biggest arithmetical miracles in the world would be required in the desert, when Moses led the people of Israel out of Egypt. Now that Moses had led the people of Israel to the desert, what was he going to do with them? They had to be fed, and feeding three or three and a half million people would require a lot of food.*

*According to the quartermaster general in the Army, Moses would have needed 1,500 tons of food each day. That much food would fill two freight trains—each a mile long.*

*Besides, you must remember they were out in the desert, and they would have needed firewood to use in cooking the food. It would take 4,000 tons of wood, a few more freight trains each a mile long just for one day. And they were forty years in transit.*

*Oh, yes, they would have needed water. If they only had enough water to drink and wash a few dishes, it would have taken 11,000,000 gallons each day—enough water to fill a freight train 1,800 miles long.*

*And then another thing! They had to get across the Red Sea, in one night. Now if they went on a narrow path, double file, the line would be 800 miles long, and would require thirty-five days and nights to get through. So there had to be a space in the Red Sea 3 miles wide, so they could walk 5,000 abreast to get over in one night.*

*Think about this: Every time they camped at the end of the day, a campground two-thirds the size of the state of Rhode Island was required, or a total of 750 square miles.*

*Do you think Moses figured all this out before he left? I think not. You see, Moses believed in God. He had faith that God was going to take care of these things for him.*

*Let us take courage; we have the same God. We think our problems are so big. Remember what God did for Moses and the people of Israel. Team up with God and your problems will be in His care. Let Him run your life and He will take care of you.*

Author Unknown

God honors our walk when we shake out the shame, doubt, and fear, and simply trust Him to provide, protect, and prove His faithfulness. Knowing this should help us walk in peace with nothing to strive over. We already have all things! First of all, trusting God's promises of who we are in him helps us to walk in purity. Secondly, purity brings us to see God. Thirdly, seeing God keeps us in peace (Phil. 4:6-9). Like Joshua, we too must rid ourselves of any self-prepared plans, formulated by Satan, and put on the peaceful shoes of warfare. If we really think about it, the undercurrents of all necessary warfare are filled with the purpose of peace. We fight from peace (assured that we are saved and secure), and we fight for peace (knowing the lost need the gospel of peace), and in Christ we fight with peace (knowing the Prince of Peace is alongside to guide us). Joshua could not go against the stronghold of Jericho in his own strength, and neither can we. He had to walk in every word given by God's commander and then ... the walls fell down.

# Day Four

# Marching Down Strongholds with Shoes of Peace

"Having …your feet shod with the preparation of the gospel of peace;"
Ephesians 6:15

How are you doing with the strongholds in your life? What "Jerichos" do your loved ones face? Hasn't Satan kept too much behind those walls for too long? Isn't it time for the walls of your Jericho to come down so that you can enter into God's Promised Land?

Let's take a look at the battle plans that God gave Joshua and his people to bring down the walls.

Read Joshua 5 and 6 carefully. Note the nouns and verbs pertaining to the people by underlining them in your Bible.

God's instructions told the priests to bear the ark and to bear trumpets and ram's horns; they were to compass and "go around the city once" a day for six days and on the seventh day they were to go around seven times, blow the ram's horn, blow the trumpet, and shout for victory (Joshua 6:3-4).

How many times were the people to go around each day? _____

How many times were the people to go around the seventh day? _____

Did you write once for each day and seven on the seventh day? That was a lot of prayer walking, wasn't it? Surely it was a different plan from the one they would have chosen, but it was the right plan.

Can you remember a time when God placed it on your heart to do something that was out of the ordinary? If so, take some time to record that here.

_____

_____

The first experience we will encounter when coming up against Satan's ground is a well-fortified wall—a stronghold. Strongholds consist of a set way of thinking in our minds, as well as in the minds of those we love. Our enemy doesn't intend for anyone to step inside this territory or claim this ground. Yet it is truly not his ground. In his book *Reclaiming Surrendered Ground*, Jim Logan teaches us that the only ground the enemy has in a Christian's life is what we yield to him.[2] It is our promised land and it is time we reclaim it. It will not be easy. It will take time and dedication. The walls of his strongly held city (stronghold) are nearly as thick as they are high. Yet, just as the inhabitants of Jericho, he trembles in insecurity. He knows that Our God is with us. Satan has heard the prayers of mothers and sisters; he has been informed of the crossing of our Jordan. He has heard of the feats of faith. He knows he is defeated, and he sits vulnerable—"shut up in Jericho" (Joshua 5:1 and Joshua 6:1). So come now children of God, let us take out the battle plan of old and by this take down the walls, setting at naught Satan's strongholds.

Look at the following battle plan for bringing down a stronghold.

Although this was a literal plan of attack used by Joshua, it is there for us as a spiritual plan of battle as well.

**Battle plans for bringing down strongholds (Joshua 5 and 6):**

1. Surrender your life - Surrender your plans fully to God.
2. Step over your Jordan - Follow God by faith. Step into the waters of tomorrow with full surrender and trust. The moment the sole of your foot touches the water of faith, you will walk over on dry ground.

3. Sanctify your heart - Go to your Gilgal and cut away any impure pursuit that holds you apart from God.

4. Submit your ways - Ask God for his battle plans in dealing with your problems (your Jericho).

5. <u>Show your trust in God</u>

   Realize God's ways are not our ways. Be ready for His plan to be different from yours.

6. <u>Steady your imaginations</u>
   Realize that it takes time to bring down a wall—keep walking.

7. <u>Seek God's presence</u>

   Keep your eye on the ark of God's protection, provision, and promise.

   See Aaron's budding rod and know that Jesus is our priest who will rule and protect you.

   Look up to the mercy seat and remember Christ's blood declares that you are richly loved.

8. <u>Sojourn together in peace.</u>

   Continue your daily walk with God. Walk quietly around your problems in prayer and hear the priest of heaven blow the trumpet of victory.

9. <u>Shout in praise</u>. Declare in your heart that God will win the war.

   Be prepared to enter your promised land of peace with your God. He is faithful who has promised!

10. <u>Sanctify the first spoils of battle to God</u> (the first fruits = His tithe) Lay all the goods won from your Jericho battles at His feet.

# Day Five

# Mark It Of; Claim It!

"Every place that the sole of your foot shall tread upon, that have I given unto you, as I said unto Moses." Joshua 1:3

Our last lesson this week has us putting on the shoes of warfare and claiming promised ground. We dare not trust our own heart. Instead, we must stand on the word of God. Joshua's background as a trained warrior didn't assure victory with Jericho. Even the best Christian must seek God in bringing down a stronghold. However, with God's shoes of warfare, we can walk in peace while seeing walls fall down around us. In confronting Jericho, the Israelites walked around the city and fasted from their own works. It wasn't their strength that brought down the city, and it will not be ours. Remove those boots of self-reliance and put them aside. Take up God's shoes of warfare, fellow soldier, and watch him bring down your mightiest strongholds.

When we step out by faith, God has great plans for the shoes of warfare. Surprisingly, these boots are not just for fighting. Once we win the battle, we are told to put these shoes right back on and walk over all the land that we want to possess. What does this mean? It means facing some giants in order to claim our ground. It's not easy. Those giants of fear and insecurity seem unapproachable, don't they? I am counseling a friend right now who spends many of her days fighting anxiety. The giants of loneliness and insignificance taunt her throughout each day, she longs for someone who would love her enough to make it all go away, but the truth is she must face her own giants. As a Christian lady of God, the insecurities and lies are on her land, and she must stand in Christ wearing the shoes of warfare and fighting out the battle. Only then will she be free to enjoy the love of another. Dependence on others only imprisons us to our Jerichos. Dependence on God helps us to not only bring down the walls of our Jericho, but to also walk over and claim our promised land. The promises are there: Joshua 1:9; Romans 8:1; Romans 8:28-38. Put on God's shoes of peace and walk in them to claim the victory over the flesh, world, and the devil. It matters what you are standing on. If we put on the shoes of faith, we can conquer.

That is just what Stanley Praimnath did. Don't recognize the name? Let me introduce you. Stanley Praimnath was a man who worked on one of the top floors of the twin towers on September 11, 2001. Stanley had a pair of shoes that he had owned for quite a while, but had not worn. He really liked the shoes and decided, on that particular day, to get them out and wear them. He thought they were nice looking. His wife thought they were hideous. The shoes had very thick soles and were somewhat different, he confessed. However, as God would arrange it, Stanley wore those unforgettable shoes on that unforgettable day. He later confessed, while recounting his story, that those unique thick-soled shoes saved his life. While miraculously making his way though the sharp metal and piercing rubble, his shoes allowed him to tread over what would have rendered him injured and unable to walk. If his feet had not been well covered, Stanley would have more than likely been rendered immobile and very possibly lost his life. He tells of praying that morning, asking God to lead him and protect him in all his ways. God did, right down to the shoes![3]

What do our shoes of peace look like? I would say they are woven with the fruit (virtues) of the spirit. I've heard it said that ancient warriors carved an image of the enemy on their shoe. The soldier then treaded on his enemy many times mentally and symbolically under his feet before literally treading him down.

What enemy would you draw on the bottom of your shoes of peace? Note that I asked *what*, not *who*. Our warfare is against our own fleshly lusts, worldly enticements, and the temptations of the devil. Although Satan often works through others, we are not focusing on the offenses of others; we are going to the root of the problem. Our enemies are most often things such as fear, pride, greed, and selfishness. Which of these would you draw on the bottom of your shoes of peace? List them below.

_____

_____

In the space provided, draw the outline of a shoe. Then draw a symbol of your enemy on the bottom of your shoe.

God gave Joshua and the children of Israel the right shoes to walk over their promised land. The claims were open to as much as they would claim. Keep in mind "claim" here involved some battles. It wasn't the idea of "Ready, Set, Go"... Okay, Joshua, see how far you can walk today and everywhere you leave a footprint is yours. No, it wasn't that easy, friend. "Claim" here involved intentional taking. The giants have it, but we are taking it back! It is that kind of claim. This gives a whole new dimension to prayer walking, does it not? Every step is set forth in faith—not footprints of retreat, but footprints of a steady soldier. These footprints testified of a forward advancement of a mighty army.

Take time to read Joshua 1:3 and Joshua 3:13

How do these verses emphasize the need to step out in faith? _____

_____

_____

Note: The significant claims here are not for temporary worldly goods as we often hear from "name it and claim it" speakers. Instead, we can make claims on the fruits of the Spirit such as: love, joy, peace, longsuffering, gentleness, patience, and self-control. We can have victory in the battlefield of our mind. Underline the word "tread" in Joshua 1:3. Our claiming requires faith with shoe leather, obeying the things God has placed in front of us to do. For Joshua this meant conquering the city of Jericho and claiming the Promised Land. Our goal is similar yet a bit different. Joshua claimed physical ground; we are to claim spiritual ground.

God leads me in these battles in my own life, and these claims always include giants. As my commander, He leads right on past giant footprints, and we stalk the giants right off the promised ground. I usually don't go voluntarily. As a matter of fact, I want to go back to camp! My mind tells me—I can't do this! However, God leads on, and my great commander says to me, "Come, my child, these are the giants from days of old. Remember the ones you first saw when looking over the land of promise. They are the ones who kept your people away from claiming my promise. It's time -Time to face your giants. This is the land I have granted you. However, you must face them, and you must reclaim it. I am with you. Just remember to look at me and not the giant. Soon they will be gone, and you will rest."

# WEEK FOUR

## Wedding Shoes

# Day One

## With This Shoe, I Thee Wed

"Now this was the manner in former Israel concerning redeeming and
concerning changing, for to confirm all things;
a man plucked off his shoe, and gave it to his neighbor:
and this was a testimony in Israel" Ruth 4:**7**

When God joins two lives together, there is an amazing
testimony behind their union. As I mentioned
previously, I enjoy hearing how couples first meet. In
fact, I usually end up sharing my own story in return, and I always
enjoy reflecting on how God joined my path with that of my husband.
Our story is a bit different. "Love at first sight" would not be the way I
would describe it. It was more like faith with no sight. You see, Billy
and I met on a blind date. I had heard his voice by phone, but had
never spoken to him face-to-face. It kind of makes you think of our
relationship with the Lord. We speak to Him now, and He speaks to
us, yet one day we will see Him face-to-face.

Let me back up and give you a little more background on our
meeting. I had been in a relationship with a good Christian guy for
quite some time and when it ended, my heart was broken. I confessed
to God that I did not want to trust my heart in any further relationships.
I even asked the Lord to put a stop to any relationship that was not in
His will. "Don't let me have over one date with anyone, Lord, unless it

is the one you choose for me," I prayed. God answered my prayers just as I had asked, and after one long year of brief encounters, I was ready to give up. Evidently, I was not to marry. *Maybe I am cut out to be a single missionary instead*, I thought.

My college roommate, Robin, and I were in our dorm room one weekend "singing the blues." Her sad story was that the guy she had dated for years was never going to propose. "I'm never going to get a ring," she said in frustration. I turned to her and replied, "A ring? Are you kidding? I am never going to have more than one date!" However, our blues turned to laughter and within days, she was given a ring, and I had received a phone call from a mystery man.

The note on my "fancy dancy" dry erase board read—"Billy Howell called—said he will call back later." Billy Howell??? The only Howells I had heard of starred on Gilligan's Island. Billy Howell—I wondered if this young man might be one of those "preacher boys" who attended Bible College with my dad. Dad had told our family hilarious stories about these ministerial students. He said they would run up and down the dormitory hallway practicing their sermons and even have "rapture practice" as they made their jumps in mid-stride of their run. To make a long story short—Billy was one of the guys from Clear Creek Bible College. However, he was not one of the ones who did the running leaps or set an alarm clock at 5:00 a.m. only to let the alarm blare on and on until my Dad knocked on their door to give them a Lazarus type call to "Come forth" from the dead. Okay, maybe it was more like, "Hey, get up and turn that clock off, boy!" (Dad was there two days a week finishing up his degree, and so was blessed to get to know the boys) One day, Billy saw Dad working on his car and offered to help. I call it the "Eliezer-watering-the-camel approach." (Remember Eliezer, Abraham's servant who went out to find a wife for his son, Isaac? Eliezer chose Rebecca because of her generous heart – Genesis 24.) After offering to help with Dad's "camel," Billy asked Dad to tell everyone in his family "Hello." He had heard a little about me, and was hinting for an open door. Dad's response was, "Some things—you have to do for yourself." That was all Billy needed. He got my phone number, came over, and after one ... then two dates, I knew he must be Mr. Right! The prayer hold of "no more than one date" had lifted, so I felt sure this must be my approved prince charming. I was so happy! The people around me probably thought I was having rapture practice. He most definitely was God's choice, and is, Mr. Right. Now, over twenty years later, we hold to our commitment to Christ and to each other as the foundation of our marriage. Our promises made before God are real and binding. My husband is my best friend, provider, protector, and the spiritual leader of our home. While my heart was once broken by a lost commitment, it has been redeemed by one who has claimed me by his promised word of covenant.

There is a story in scripture of another couple who met unexpectedly, or so they thought. In reality, God had planned their union. That couple is none other than Ruth and Boaz. The book of Ruth starts out on a sad note. Ruth lost her husband by death; however, she walked through this time with total dedication to her mother-in-law. She vowed to follow her mother-in-law, Naomi, and Naomi's God. While working hard to survive, God sent Ruth to a place where she would meet her kinsman redeemer. Unexpectedly and amazingly, God came to Naomi and Ruth during their darkest times, and brought them light.

Many of us are familiar with the book of Ruth. The timeless love story of Ruth and Boaz gives us a beautiful picture of romance and redemption. What begins with a funeral ends with a wedding and a special birth. This interesting real life narrative is filled with amazing details. One detail, in particular, connects us with our continuing study of shoes in scripture—the wedding shoe. The shoe in the passage of Ruth is all about Covenant.

In chapter four of Ruth, we see a simple sandal used as a symbol. The lesson in this symbol of the shoe is simply to keep your commitments. Do what you say you will do (James 5:12). Keep your word. How appropriate and fitting to hold forth a shoe to tie up a promise of the soul. That is what the Jewish man did in the former courts of Israel. Symbolic visual aids were an important part of ancient Jewish teaching, as they still are today. The use of an object in a lesson helps to drive a point home to the heart and mind of man. Advertisers of our day are very wise to this fact. Great amounts of time and money are invested each day in order to leave an impression on our mind. Throughout our day, we are bombarded with images that influence us, sometimes without even being aware of them.

While the use of symbols is no new discovery, it is best seen and appreciated when observed in God's Word. Our God and Creator designed our mind to take in information audibly and visibly, thus leaving a colorful imprint to be used later. He thoughtfully planned for us to have images to emphasize the lessons of life. Our Lord determined that strong images would be used to nail down the serious commands, while humble forms would be used to represent love and commitment. One of these symbols of promise and honor seen in the book of Ruth is a simple sandal. A wedding shoe, if you will, that signifies responsibility, stewardship, and dedication. When a Jewish man held up his shoe among the witnesses and elders at the city gate, he was saying, "I transfer my rights of ownership of this person or property." He would then give the shoe to the one who would like to purchase the land or item to be claimed. By taking the sandal, the new overseer committed to care for, and be responsible for, that which he purchased. We see the shoe used to signify a promised word as we read in the following Bible verse, "Now this was the manner in former Israel concerning redeeming and concerning changing, for to confirm all things; a man plucked off his shoe, and gave it to his neighbor: and this was a testimony in Israel." Ruth 4:7

The shoe in the book of Ruth was a binding contract. As we read in the previous scripture (Ruth 4:7), it was a symbol of commitment, exchange, and confirmation. The cut of leather that a man stood on was a sign of his testimony. It represented what he claimed, or what he gave up right to. Holding up the shoe was a visual proclamation of a transaction. Ownership was transferred as the shoe was passed from the one relinquishing his right to the new owner or overseer. It proclaimed in a visual form what one promised to do. The Jewish man of God was to be a representation of God's character, and God always stands on what He says. He is always true to His word.

This account in Ruth is like a picture of God, Himself, receiving a shoe from the law. The law could not redeem us and had to surrender its right to Jesus, our Kinsman redeemer. We can see our Savior taking the shoe in order to redeem the name of the deceased. We were dead in sin, yet He paid the ultimate price at Calvary's cross to bring us to life.

Take time to stop and read through the book of Ruth. There are only four small chapters, and it will be an eternal investment. Write down any thoughts or questions as you read. Take a journey back through time. Travel with Elimelech from Bethlehem and then down to Moab. Respectfully pause to grieve with Naomi, Orpah, and Ruth at the graves of their loved ones. Take the rugged road with Naomi and Ruth back to Bethlehem. Finally, glean with Ruth in the fields of Boaz, and then follow her to her wedding in Bethlehem. Maybe you

could even listen in as the women of Bethlehem decide what to name
Ruth's baby boy (Ruth 4:17). Enjoy! Oh, and take a shovel and spade.
You just may uncover a shoe.

Ruth1

_____

_____

_____

_____

_____

Ruth 2

_____

_____

_____

_____

_____

Ruth 3

_____

_____

_____

_____

_____

## Ruth 4

_____

_____

_____

_____

_____

# Day Two

# Removing Shoes of Insecurity

I hope you enjoyed your walk through the life of Ruth. Do you have any questions? If so, jot them down for further study.

Personal questions on the book of Ruth:

_____

_____

_____

The following are some ideas to help you dig deeper to answer your questions:

- Pray over your question—ask God to reveal the meaning of His Word to you.
- Ask your husband about your question.
- Ask a well-studied Christian woman about them.
- Seek out similar verses in the Bible (cross references).
- Begin reading books about Bible manners and customs.

Now, let's look together at this heart-warming love story, shall we? It was harvest time in Bethlehem, and harvest was no doubt celebrated with much rejoicing, especially since the famine and drought that Naomi had experienced when last here in Bethlehem. Yet what did Naomi have to celebrate? Not only did drought from the land make her life difficult, but a drought from her soul also seemed to dry up any hope of harvesting joy. Naomi and Ruth were forced to put on the widows' shoes of insecurity. It was not something they chose or understood. Instead, circumstances seemed to bring this chapter to them uninvited. However, as we will see, God had some beautiful shoes ready for these two ladies who had been made vulnerable by death. To these frail ones, God extended promise and protection through the covenant coverings of wedding shoes. They would soon exchange their dark wrappings of mourning for beautiful wedding shoes of celebration.

Naomi, her husband, and two sons, Mahlon and Chilion, had gone *down* to Moab—immoral, idol-worshipping Moab. The Jews had been instructed to stay separated from these pagan people. Going down to Moab to find bread would prove costly to Naomi's family. They would face more than hunger in Moab, for Naomi's husband and two sons would die there. Moab, called God's wash pot in other scriptures, was an ungodly place. In Ruth 1:1, we can find that Elimelech had only planned to "sojourn" there, yet after his death, his sons married and dwelt in Moab until their own death. Leaving Bethlehem, the house of bread, when its baskets were empty proved to be a fatal decision. Yet God, in His mercy, would remember Naomi. He would also have mercy to continue the name of the deceased.[1]

Oh, the sweet mercy of our God! He works all things for good in the life of a believer (Romans 8:28). This was true in the Old Testament, as it is in the New Testament. Even after Elimelech had failed to trust God to provide during hard times, God extended amazing grace. God didn't hold a grudge for seeking refuge in the enemy's camp, He had compassion, for when Naomi returned, God blessed! Upon coming back to the house of bread, God showered His mercies on Naomi, Ruth, and even on the name of the deceased to honor them. However, Naomi would not see God' redemptive plan at first. Returning to Bethlehem all seemed bleak for Naomi. She still waded through much grief. "Call me Mara" (bitter) was her reply to those greeting her by "Naomi". Yet, as Naomi pulled the shade down on any ray of light, Ruth stepped out into the day to gather grain from Bethlehem.

Ruth's concern was not for herself, but for her mother-in-law, Naomi. She disregarded her own need for new spiritual shoes, and only saw the need for her mother-in-law, Naomi. Bro. Jerry Lowry, Pastor from my college days, once shared in a sermon that if you feel discouraged, go out and help another. In other words, one remedy for grief is giving. In doing so, you forget your own troubles and rejoice in helping another. Ruth went forward, with a thankful heart, to serve Naomi. This former Moabitess was not cast down for what she did not have, but instead she was eternally grateful for what she did have. Although Ruth, too, had lost much, what she had found was more sustaining than her loss. This former stranger and pagan had found the Lord God Jehovah. As a Moabite, Ruth had known what it was like to feel lost and undone. She had known emptiness and fear. Yet now, she had come to find acceptance in Naomi's one true God. And Naomi's God was now her God. We see Ruth's humble confession back in Ruth1:16 (I love that verse. I used it in my wedding vows). Ruth felt acceptance in Naomi's God, and Ruth would cling to this newfound love and acceptance in Jehovah God. She would take him as her God as well.

I recently attended a special graveside service. After my husband concluded his comments at the graveside, he asked for any other words from the family. One lady shared a special testimony about the comfort of belonging. She spoke of how her deceased aunt would always welcome, love, and encourage those who entered her home. Meeting family and friends on the front porch with loving affections, she made them all feel absolutely accepted. This niece went on to say that coming into her husband's family was the beginning of understanding what a close family really was. She confessed she had not known this type of love before. With tears in her eyes, she vowed to live her life as the deceased aunt had. Loving others in a personal way would be a part of her life as well. With a broken heart, she acknowledged thankfulness for being loved in such a warm and personal way. My mind went directly to Ruth. How special it must have been to be brought out of pagan Moab and into a place of belonging. Acceptance by God and purpose now filled Ruth's heart. Not even death had tainted her thankfulness. Ruth walked on in shoes of service to Naomi and to Naomi's God. She wanted to hold to this security and closeness she had found through Naomi's witness.

As Ruth went on with thankfulness to the fields to glean, her heart was filled with dedication and service. One day, Ruth came to the fields of one named Boaz to gather from the corners of his land. As a widow, she had a God-ordained right by the Jewish law to gather extra grain from nearby fields. This was an arranged act of charity that Jews mandated in order to provide food for the needy. By God's guidance, Ruth gathered grain in the field of Boaz. It is very interesting to know that Boaz was either the son or the grandson of Rahab (scholars differ). Remember Rahab? She was another pagan and foreigner brought in to find refuge in God (Joshua 6:25). Are you seeing a divine, heavenly hand painting a back drop here? What a special backdrop it is, too! God's love stories are far better than any make-believe fairy tale. This was a real prince charming claiming an unlikely bride, and by way of a real slipper. Destiny was coming to the desolate. The unexpecting poor one would be claimed by the wealthy one by way of a shoe.

With her mind on gleaning, Ruth was unaware that Boaz had noticed her, but he had! As a matter of fact, the master of the land had not only noticed her, but he had been gathering some grain himself. Boaz had reaped important information about this one called Ruth. He had harvested an abundance of joyful news that painted a picture of a beautiful serving woman. He learned of Ruth's dedication and service, and he admonished her.

As I once heard Dr. Adrian Rogers say in a message, Boaz spoke first. He came to Ruth as she gathered grain and invited her to come to his table. He encouraged her to remain in his fields and to glean there continually. He even had instructed his men to drop handfuls out to her on purpose. As Ruth ate at the table with Boaz, he fellowshipped with her and blessed her. Later, while Ruth shared the news with her mother-in-law, a ray of light dawned in Naomi's heart. Boaz was a near kinsman! Naomi began to see God's hand of grace and mercy, and she joined in. She told Ruth to present herself quietly and humbly at the feet of Boaz. Ruth obeyed, washing and anointing herself with fragrance. Ruth went to the threshing floor where the men were sleeping to guard their grain. There in the night, Ruth quietly lay down at the feet of Boaz. When Boaz awakened, Ruth identified herself and confessed her need to be taken in and redeemed. It was an accepted custom of that day for a widow to ask a near kinsman to take her in. Take a moment to read the Levirate law.

"If brethren dwell together, and one of them die, and have no child, the wife of the dead shall not marry without unto a stranger: her husband's brother shall go in unto her, and take her to him to wife, and perform the duty of an husband's brother unto her. And it shall be, that the firstborn which she beareth shall succeed in the name of his brother which is dead, that his name be not put out of Israel. And if the man like not to take his brother's wife, then let his brother's wife go up to the gate unto the elders, and say, My husband's brother refuseth to raise up unto his brother a name in Israel, he will not perform the duty of my husband's brother. Then the elders of his city shall call him, and speak unto him: and if he stand to it, and say, I like not to take her; then shall his brother's wife come unto him in the presence of the elders, and loose his shoe from off his foot, and spit in his face, and shall answer and say, So shall it be done unto that man that will not build up his brother's house. And his name shall be called in Israel, The *house of him that hath his shoe loosed*." Deuteronomy 25:5-10

Deuteronomy 25: 7-10 states that if a brother would not claim his brother's widow, the widow then had the right to unloose his shoe and spit in his face. It was a shameful thing not to stand on commitment. The punishment in this scripture was to be shamed—by not only a spit in the face, but also a shameful labeling. If the nearest male relative did not marry the widow, he was looked down upon. Anyone not caring for his brother's widow and redeeming the name of the dead was to be called "the house of the *loosed shoe*." The poor were not to be forsaken, and the dead were not to be forgotten. God cares in detail about His people. The Levirate law was ordained by God and written into the books to secure the poor, needy, and the name of the deceased. The widow, fatherless, and those gone on in death needed to be spoken for.

What a beautiful picture of our redemption and salvation. We come like Ruth hungry, in poverty, and seeking food. Our redeemer speaks inviting us to come, gather, and feast. He invites us to provision. We then come to his feet and humbly ask for covering and redemption. Seeing that the law cannot purchase us, our redeemer claims us. Jesus steps forth and accepts the shoe of relinquishment from the law. We are claimed. Wedding shoes are given—vows made—blessings spoken, and we are taken in. The name of the dead is continued, and hope is born. The shoe is filed as the document of claim, and an eternal symbol of ownership testifies to our new identity. What the law could not do, Jesus did! Good works could not save me, keeping the rules would not do it. The law could only stand and confess, "I cannot redeem—she would mar and pollute my image." Like Ruth, we are pagans coming to be redeemed, and we have the most wonderful redeemer of all in Jesus.

At graveside services, my husband sometimes reads a poem that makes me think of the Levirate law. I think you will appreciate it.

### *How to Remember Me*

*A time will come when my life will cease,*
*But when that time comes I ask that you remember these things:*
*Bury my body but don't bury my beliefs.*
*Bury my heart but don't bury my love.*
*Bury my eyes but not my vision.*

*Bury my feet but not the path of my life.*

*Bury my hands but don't bury my diligent efforts.*

*Bury my shoulders but not the concerns I carried.*

*Bury my voice but not my message.*

*Bury my mind but don't bury my dreams.*

*Bury me but don't bury my life.*

*If you must bury something let it be my faults and my weaknesses,*

*But let my life continue on in you.*

-Author unknown

# Day Three

## Putting on God's Shoes of Covenant

"Know ye therefore that the Lord thy God, he is God, the faithful God, which keepeth covenant and mercy with them that love him and keep his commandments to a thousand generations." Deuteronomy 7: 9

God cares much about commitments. His desire for us is to be: redeemed, as with Ruth; encouraged, as with Naomi; and remembered, as in the lives of Mahlon and Chilion. James 1:27 states, "Pure religion and undefiled before God and the Father is this, to visit the fatherless and widows in their affliction, and to keep himself unspotted from the world."

One day Jesus will declare to the righteous, "For I was a hungered, and ye gave me meat: I was thirsty, and ye gave me drink: I was a stranger, and ye took me in" (Matthew 25:35). By our word we will be judged, as well as by our actions. Are we true to our word? Are our words set forth in actions? Are we telling the lonely and afraid where to find shoes? Many poor barefoot souls long for the shoes of covenant.

Many don't stress the importance of keeping their word in our day and age. Little time is spent in remorse over unkept vows. Instead, many move from one quickly given and broken promise to another. Disregarding a covenant is not only accepted, but it is also promoted.

Sometime ago, I saw a billboard that boldly read: Divorce—$495.00. Sadly, this is what we have come to—quick, cheap ways to get out of a vow. However, the Christian home should not be known as "the house of the loose shoe" as was the unwilling kinsman in the book of Ruth. Before we make a promise, we should prayerfully wait until God says "Yes" to the decision. Upon giving our word of commitment, we are then to make any sacrifices necessary to keep that vow. Covenants always require sacrifice.

Several questions go through my mind as I wonder how we have strayed so far from being a covenant people. For example, why are our vows so easily severed? Why do some live immorally, not caring to make a vow at all? Are relationships special? Is our word really our word? Are promises really promises?

In recent times, there is a vagrant denial of conviction and consequences in relationship to covenant breaking. The word "promise" for many has a watered down meaning that is more like quicksand than a rock of security. Many make vows at the altar, and they soon alter their vows. It is hard to believe, but there really was a time when your word was your word. Promises were kept and vows were cherished, both to God and to one another. This was the case with Boaz—he considered his word and kept his word. When he accepted the commitment of the wedding shoe, he stood on it.

Why is it so important to use caution in giving a promise? And why is it so vital that we keep our "yes" as "yes" and our "no" as "no"? (Matthew 5:37) We should keep our word because we are to represent God's ways to a needy world. We are his ambassadors, reflections of his character, and his holy nature. Others look to us to see a picture of what God is like. They listen to us to learn if God keeps his word. We stand to exemplify the great covenant keeper and his relationship to his church. When we keep our word, others trust that Christ keeps his word. All of us fail at one time or another to keep our word. Whether it was by over commitment, good intentions, or just neglect, we have and will fall short. However, others should see a conviction and repentance when we do. Eyewitnesses should be able to confess that our word is valuable to us. A lost and dying world longs to see safe havens of commitment.

How are you doing on holding you commitments as precious? I will confess I have failed. How about you, friend? Are you like Naomi and coming back to the house of bread? Are you thankful as Ruth and expressing it by thinking of another before yourself? Are we gracious, like Boaz, as he gave plentifully to the needy and forsaken? Are we like our heavenly father honoring those who have gone on before by continuing their good work? How about at home? Are we keeping our covenants? Are our words first considered then kept?

Assignment of the day: Make a list of widows in your church and neighborhood. Commit to pray over them, and then put leather to your prayer by way of a visit, phone call, or handwritten note. As a church outreach, consider helping a widow financially who may be without children or family to support her. They need to know that God is a keeper of the widow and a Father to the fatherless. We are God's vessels of service on this earth. Let's allow God's love to flow through us as we display the shoes of covenant to those feeling barefoot and barren.

Pray list for widows:

_____

_____

_____

Now make a list of single mothers. This is a group that is often overlooked and heavy burdened.

_____

_____

_____

God's Word tells us to do all things by prayer. Let's pray, too, this week for those struggling to keep their covenant promise in their marriage. We need one another's prayer support. As you adopt a widow, ask God to send you a young couple or so to watch over, love, mentor, and cover in prayer as well. We have a part to do in God's shoe department. Shoes of covenant are to be displayed and extended through our life.

Dear Lord,

Please help us to hold to the shoe of covenant and present to the world the witness of a word considered, and a promise kept, as we hold forth the wedding shoe of covenant.

In the name of, Jesus, our covenant keeper,

Amen.

# Day Four

## Shoes of Beauty

"I clothed thee also with broidered work,
and shod thee with badger's skin…"
Ezekiel 16:10

The wedding shoes of covenant not only give a safe covering, but they also offer a covering of beauty. Perhaps the most beautiful accent to the spiritual bride's shoes is the adornment of peace. A peace that gives hope is a radiant cloud to walk upon.

Peace is important in any covenant relationship. The fear that one will be abandoned or rejected can lead to feelings of desperate emotion and dependent behavior. A desperate person longs to wear peace, but instead wears shoes more like cleats. Their spikes sink into every relationship they touch with a painful hold. What a beautiful virtue the Lord selected when choosing peace to represent our walk.

Describe the difference in the actions of a peace-filled person and an anxious, dependent soul.

_____

_____

_____

_____

Walking in peace is a progressive act. Peace leads to hope. When our heart can safely trust then it can also hope. Life is full of conflicts, losses, and disappointments. We can't cling to people or things, but we can love them when we know that our foundational acceptance is in Christ alone. Hope that comes from peace will sustain us during difficult and lonely times.

Separation is heart–wrenching, especially when there is distance between a husband and wife. The Jewish ladies of old were familiar with separation. From the time they were espoused, their bridegroom was off and away building an addition to his father's house. The bride's job was being well prepared while she waited and hoped for the groom's return. When he did return (usually at midnight), she was to be found prepared for her new life. What drove this young woman and her maidens to be constantly prepared? Hope based on the peace of her promise that her bridegroom would return. She was to sleep with her shoes of peace ready at all times. While the bride waited, she was always to be faithful to her covenant of her engagement.

In Ezekiel 16, God speaks through Ezekiel to give a picture of a husband covering his bride with beauty. One of the coverings he provided for her was the shoes made from badger's skin. In Bible times, badger's skin was the best material that could be found to construct a shoe. Here we see in the Old Testament illustration of Ezekiel 16, a touching picture of how God provides the best coverings for our walk. As God's redeemed children, we can walk in the beauty of peace. We are daughters of the King, and we can walk in his confidence. When we put on these beautiful shoes, others will be drawn to God. In Proverbs 31:11, the peace of a godly wife drew her husband to "safely trust in her," then too in the wisdom writings of Song of Solomon, the bridegroom proclaimed, "How beautiful are thy feet with shoes, O prince's daughter!" Song of Solomon 7:1 (a)

Sadly, the bride in Ezekiel 16 would be unfaithful. Though the groom had decked her in the most durable and beautiful coverings, she later turned to pagans for new attention and admiration. Contentment left her, and a greed for more and more attention to her beauty consumed her. She failed to walk with her husband in the shoes of covenant and became a desperate slave to desired attention from another.

Let's look for today at the lady of Proverbs 31: 10-31. List the virtues of beauty this woman of covenant exhibits throughout her daily life.

_____

_____

_____

_____

"We can tell a lot about a person from their shoes," as one of the ladies in my shoe studies exclaimed. As women, we are drawn to beauty. This is probably due to the fact that God created us to be vessels of beauty.

# Day Five

## Shoes of Endurance

"Thy shoes shall be iron and brass;
and as thy days, so shall thy strength be."
Deuteronomy 33:25

Shoes are a big deal to us. We want our shoes to match our purse and clothes. We want new shoes and comfortable shoes, but if you are like me, I have realized one of the most important things to consider in shoes is their quality of endurance. Yes, we want beauty, but it is best if it is nicely joined with durability.

Confession—I'm sure I have permanent damage to my right foot due to the fact that I sacrificed shoes of endurance for dressy heels. I had planned on a fun-filled day to Biltmore in Asheville, North Carolina, with our high school students and fellow teachers. However, the fun was interrupted by painful feet about midway through our day. The worst part was—I knew better! I tossed around the thoughts of just wearing some casual flats, but the black and white heels were much cuter. Needless to say, the heels won in the battle of decision and my feet lost in the battle of comfort. These days, I find myself looking for cute flats.

Covenants aren't meant to be detestable; they are meant to provide security and comfort. My husband sometimes shares "humorous illustrations" during his sermon delivery. (Some of those nearly get him bologna for lunch over roast and potatoes—not really, we just pick at each other.) For example, one of his "funnies" goes as follows: "A man is not complete, until he is married ... then ... he is finished!" (Bologna, right? Doesn't that one deserve a bologna sandwich?) Though we may joke about the trials of marriage, we both hold well to the beautiful, safe, enduring strength of our covenant relationship in Christ. Individually, as a couple, and as a family, we stand in the shoes of peace knowing the everlasting arms of God's grace holds us and will never leave us. Any relationship has its battles for endurance, thus the previous joke. For many, the trials of relationships seem too hard to endure; however, we are to be there as Christians showing forth the strong shoes of endurance. God promised the children of Israel shoes of endurance when they walked with Him in the desert. "And I have led you forty years in the wilderness: your clothes are not waxen old upon you, and thy shoe is not waxen old upon thy foot" (Deuteronomy 29:5). Let's spend some time in Deuteronomy for just a bit. You are going to love this.

In Deuteronomy, we see a verse first to the tribe of Asher, but true to us as well, "Thy shoes shall be iron and brass; and as thy days, so shall thy strength be" (Deuteronomy 33:25). Although we have looked at this verse in a previous day of study, I want us to see it again. (Repetition is a great teacher.) One of my mentors and dear mothers in the Lord, Betty Asher, holds to this verse daily, and especially in difficult times. God's Word of endurance has held her through the sudden loss of her son and husband. She wears God's shoes of endurance so beautifully. Another dear mentor and mother in the Lord, Joan Foley, bears a similar testimony. She too lost a son, and has experienced the trials of life, yet she stands strong in the shoes of endurance. These two ladies, along with my sweet, godly mother are among my greatest earthly role models. I love them all three, and I am amazed at how they wear the strong shoes of iron and brass so faithfully.

Looking back at this verse in Deuteronomy 33:25, describe what this promise says to you.

_____

_____

_____

_____

Find Deuteronomy 33:26-28 in your Bible. This is one you will want to highlight. What a sweet promise of endurance. Write out the promises of these verses.

_____

_____

_____

_____

Did you see in Deut. 33:26 that as the things that fly across the sky, God quickly responds to our call? In verse 27, His eternal qualities of refuge are pointed out, and there in 27-28 we see a most beautiful picture of our God sweeping us in His arms and thrusting the enemy away to destruction. Everlastingly kept—I love it!

I was given a story of enduring shoes by a thoughtful friend named Vicky.

Our shoes make a difference. In this story, a wife tells of her husband, Rick, and how his shoes made all the difference in his endurance.

### God's Cleats

*My husband grew up with a single mother, and very little money. In high school, Rick wanted to try out for track and field—he dreamed of running fast and long, and throwing a javelin. The problem was he didn't have the right shoes, and couldn't afford them. Thank God for good friends and a kind coach.*

*One of Rick's close friends invited Rick over to his house one day and said, "Try these running shoes on. They just don't fit my feet right and I'll never wear them." Rick wasn't sure if J.T. was telling the truth, but the shoes fit Rick fine. Those shoes helped him qualify for the state meet in the 800-meter race. Running shoes allowed Rick to run much faster than his old sneakers would, but he would slip and slide in them while trying to throw the javelin. One day after practice, Rick's coach called him over and held up a big box of cleats. "Here are some unclaimed shoes students left in the lockers at the end of the school year. Find your size if you can." Rick found some that fit and the cleats made all the difference. Even the "crunching" sound they made on the track sent shivers of confidence and purpose up Rick's spine. Rick discovered it's much easier to strive for the goal when your footing is secure.[2]*

-Rachel Olsen

When we have the assurance that our feet are kept, we have peace. Peace leads to hope and hope walks forward in grace with shoes of endurance.

Spend time this week committing the following verse to memory:

"Let your conversation be without covetousness; and be content with such things as ye have; for he hath said, I will never leave thee, nor forsake thee." Hebrews 13:5

# WEEK FIVE

## Walking Shoes

# Day One

# Faith Walks with God

"And he commanded them that they should take nothing for this journey, save a staff only; no scrip, no bread, no money in their purse; but be shod with sandals; and not put on two coats." Mark 6:8

I n the above passage, Jesus is speaking to his disciples. He commanded them to go out with no scrip, no money, and with no extra clothing. Our Lord instructed them to take only two items: a staff and shoes. Here in Mark 6:8-9 God gives us charge as well. We are to go forward in faith and watch Him supply. As we study this truth, please note that I am not encouraging a lesson in sitting idly by while waiting for others to bring in our needs. It is a lesson in guidance and trusting God to supply for us. Consider this charge to go out empty and to watch God supply. In II Corinthians 5:7, we are compelled to "walk by faith, not by sight." Consider the connection between the words "disciple" and "discipline." The followers of Christ must learn the disciplines of their leader.

When Jesus called his disciples, they were to follow immediately. We see in Mark 6: 8-9 that not only were they to follow by faith when called, but these pilgrims were to continue to walk by faith every day– holding only to the staff of God's word and being shod only with the walking shoes of faith.

Compare and contrast Mark 6:8-9 to Matthew 10:10.

How are these verses alike?

_____

_____

How are the accounts different?

_____

_____

When some readers see differences in the gospel accounts, they assume a contradiction. However, parallel gospel passages do not confuse this command; they only give deeper meaning to Mark 6:8-9. If the child of God looks closely, he or she can see through the veiled scriptures. God's Word does not contradict itself; instead, it has different connecting accounts that shed light and deeper understanding into wonderful truths. Sometimes these covered and hidden truths are reserved for the true seeker. God's Word is full of buried treasures saved for the searching heart. Since heavenly wisdom is not to be trampled underfoot, He does not cast his pearls before swine. Believers are told to search and find. The needy are commanded to ask His Holy Spirit to illumine the way, seek, and then to knock on Heaven's door in order to have passage into his hidden wonders (Matthew 7:7).

With that in mind, we travel from Mark 6:8-9 to Matthew 10:10 and see a related account that gives needed information to Mark

6:8-9. The sandals in Mark 6:8-9 that the disciples were to take with them could very well be the light weight sandals upon their feet. These shoes could be easily put off and not weigh the traveler down. These were approved for the journey. The shoes in Matthew 10:10 referred to the shoes they were not to take. This passage could refer to shoes that would bog them down and hold them to this present world. They were not to take extra shoes, but only the ones they were wearing. In other words, they were not to take the foundations of worldly standards with them, but instead travel lightly by the faith on which they stood.

From Luke's gospel account of this occurrence (Luke 9:3), we are told not to bring any extras. Nothing to bog us down or distract us is welcomed. As Paul commends us in Hebrews 12:1, we are to "lay aside every weight and the sin which doeth so easily beset us." Only the gospel shoes of faith are needed. The sandals of faith are uniquely designed to endure the sandy paths of service. The gospel writers were all witness to these facts. While Matthew informs us on which shoes not to take (worldly foundations), Mark tells us the shoes we can take (shoes of faith), and Luke comes in with a friendly reminder to not take any extras (self-effort). We are called to hold to God's word, taking no extra staves to lean on and wearing only the shoes of faith to stand in. Extras were not needed, God would provide as they went forth in obedience. Their shoes would have a testimony of God's provisions alone. No stories of self glory were welcome.

God's call for the Israelites to walk by faith was along these same lines. The children of Egypt were told to go out quickly from Egypt. God gave them specific instructions through his servant Moses on how to go out. They were to leave in haste with shoes on their feet and with staff in hand—sound familiar? They, too, were compelled to move out by trusting only to the staff of God's Word and the walking in shoes of faith. The children of Israel did pack some nice extras, but only by God's bidding. As you read the next few sentences, take note of how the people of Israel obtained extras and why God allowed them to do so.

After all of the terrible plagues, the Egyptians were ready to see the Israelite slaves leave. The terrified people of Egypt feared for their very lives, so they were ready to give the slaves whatever they required. God's people went out with goods packed in the caravans, yet these treasures had a special purpose. The Egyptian fabric, precious metals, raiment, and fine leather would soon be asked of them. It would be needed to build the tabernacle of God. They needed not to hold on to them for selfish gain; it would only lead to burdens, misery, and hearts turned to worship the *created* over the *Creator*. Surrendering all these extras would be a test of faith, as they were challenged to live by God's staff of protection.

In his book *The Tabernacle*, Dr. M.R. DeHaan helps us to see this Old Testament lesson in walking by faith. He explains the call to exchange sight for faith as asked by God to his people. DeHaan uses an interesting and thought-provoking manner to note his findings: "Notice the words, "I shod thee with porpoise skins; this leather was for shoe leather, and now the Lord demands that they give this precious leather, plentiful in Egypt, but unobtainable in the desert, for the covering of the tabernacle in the service of God." He continues, "We can imagine Israel saying, *'But Lord, we need this leather for our shoes,'*" and the Lord seems to say, *Give me your shoe leather and I'll take care of your feet. I'll give you shoes that won't wear out.*" [1]

God kept his word to his people as they walked by faith and were led by his word. We have the witness of Deuteronomy 29:5 also bears record: "And I have led you forty years in the wilderness: your clothes are not waxen old upon you, and thy shoe is not waxen old upon your foot."

As in our other studies of shoes in the Bible, a shoe exchange is required. God called the Israelites out and instructed them to rely only on His staff and His shoes of faith. How interesting that such a similar call was given to his disciples. Take only staff and shoes. All else must be left or exchanged. Shoes of sight must be traded for shoes of faith. Earthly goods must be laid down for eternal treasures. Selfishness left behind and shoes of service strapped on. God keeps a record of those who walk by faith. Take time to read the eleventh chapter of Hebrews and note the men and women who turned aside from worldly reason and worldly goods to follow by faith, holding only to God's promises. These men and women traveled the rugged road of faith, paying great prices to do so. Not even knowing the great reward that awaited them, as we do, they followed. These heroes of the Christian walk pleased God. God was so real to them that they stepped out to follow Him in amazing ways. Each life story was personal, and each test of faith was real. They made the exchange; they traded unseen for seen, they handed over their plans for God's plans. These faithful travelers walked with God day by day and year by year. When their guide did ask for sacrificial trust, they were ready. They trusted him with their most valued treasures, and even their very life, even down to the shoes on their feet.

It's a tough decision to trade the seen for the unseen. Trusting enough to follow God without knowing any details or outcome is never easy. Yet when we know who we are yielding to, we can be assured that He is doing all for our good. Through the darkest night and most desolate desert, He is God. God is working to make all things new and beautiful in His time. The question is will we trust Him? One of my favorite illustrations on trust is "The Pearl Story," as we call it. I love to retell it to my students when teaching about trust.

### *The Pearl Necklace*

*Jenny loved her pearl. They made her feel dressed up and grown up. She wore them everywhere—Sunday school, kindergarten, even to bed. The only time she took them off was when she went swimming or had a bubble bath. Mother said if they got wet, they might turn her neck green.*

*Jenny had a very loving daddy and every night when she was ready for bed, he would stop whatever he was doing and come upstairs to read her a story. One night when he finished the story, he asked Jenny, "Do you love me?"..."Then give me your pearls."*

*"Oh, Daddy, not my pearls, but you can have my baby doll. The brand new one I got for my birthday. She is so beautiful and you can have the yellow blanket that matches her sleeper."*

*"That's okay. Sleep well. God bless you, little one. Daddy loves you." And, as always, he brushed her cheek with a gentle kiss. A few nights later when her daddy came in, Jenny was sitting on her bed with her legs crossed Indian-style. As he came close, he noticed her chin was trembling and one silent tear rolled down her cheek. "What is it, Jenny? What's the matter?" Jenny didn't say anything but lifted her little hand up to her daddy. And when she opened it, there was her little pearl necklace. With a little quiver, she finally said, "Here, Daddy. It's for you."*

*With tears gathering in his own eyes, Jenny's kind daddy reached out with one hand to take the dime-store necklace, and with the other hand, he reached into his pocket and pulled out a blue velvet case with a strand of genuine pearls and gave them to Jenny.*[2]

Author unknown

Faith surrenders the temporary for the eternal and faith exchanges the artificial for the real. Throughout scripture, the followers of God took difficult steps to walk with Him. As Ray Vander Laan describes them, "They stood in front of kings and priest, in temples, in theatres, and arenas. With calmness, they spoke His words."[3] It is very testing at times to walk with God, but faith is bold! Take up your walking shoes. Exchange the new shoes of faith for the old, insecure shoes of sight. Walk with your God in the bold coverings of faith, and trust Him for the unseen.

# Day Two

# Walking by Faith Is Exciting

"I thank my God upon every remembrance of you, always in every
prayer of mine for you all making requests with joy, for your
fellowship in the gospel from the first day until now."
Philippians 1:3-5

Thankfully as we walk the dusty roads of ministry, we have that promise that we will never walk alone. Jesus promises that he will go with us. Even the times when we do not feel that he is there, he is certainly with us. Many times he is there through his people taking care of our needs and "washing our feet." What precious memories I have of God's people taking care of our family as we have followed our Lord with only the staff of his word and the sandals of faith. Following by faith is difficult at times, but it is also exciting.

Billy, myself, and our three girls have been blessed as we have walked our journey of faith. So many sweet people of God have cared for us and taken us in as family. We have known what it is to go out without purse and trust God to provide. We have understood what it means not to carry extra "purse" and "coat". Not relying on scrip but trusting God to prepare your words is not strange to us. Trusting God for "bread" is not something new to our three teenagers. They have learned to ask their heavenly father for provisions, and they have seen him provide. God has provided as we have followed. Through faithful servants who will always be a part of our heart and ministry, we have graciously received from God's hand.

What a beautiful exchange it is to place our little grain of mustard seed into the palm of our great Heavenly Father. When we do, He smiles (Psalms 37:3). As our family has gone out without scrip, purse, coverings, or bread, I have seen God bless us far more than we could have "made it happen" for ourselves. From the time Billy and I first walked together, God has led our walk. He has blessed us with shelter, food, friendships, "scrip and purse," when we would otherwise have had none. God is amazing! While it is impossible to share them all, I would like to tell you of a few of our stories, and encourage you that it is a blessing to walk by faith.

When Billy agreed to be the pastor of the Saxton Baptist Church, it was a step of faith. We had to travel several miles every Wednesday and Sunday. He was still in Bible College, and I worked several miles from the church field. It was a small church with a huge heart. As we sacrificed time and travel, God blessed us in return. The sweet fellowship and love of our first church field will forever glow in our hearts. God blessed us in so many ways there. One favorite memory is of two elderly twin sisters that fed us on Sunday evenings, and I mean fed us! After we had our fill of a wonderful home-cooked meal, we sat with Dell and Stell to watch the Sunday evening telecast of Dr. Charles Stanley. I was expecting our first child at the time, and many times Billy would have to fill me in on the final points of Dr. Stanley's sermon. Dell, Stell, and myself often dozed after a full Sunday at church and a wonderful meal. Soon after the message began, Dell would begin the rhythm, Stell would join in, and I would complete the trio. The snores, whimpers, and ZZZSSS were in complete harmony, I'm sure. It is amazing to remember how God provided our bread!

Another unique way God met our need was by way of an obedient young man. This young college student from our church came to us and said God had laid it on his heart to buy our groceries. We were living on the church field by then. Sure enough, he came by to get our grocery list every week. We didn't want him to do this, but he insisted God placed in on his heart. Rob worked at a local grocery store and felt this was one way God wanted him to walk by faith. I tried to keep my list to a minimum, knowing that this young brother in Christ was giving in such a kind way. However, he would look over it and insist that we add more. The people of the church showered us with blessings, both materially and spiritually. They helped us with our first year as parents, and our first years as pastor and wife. When we left it was heartbreaking, for we had all tasted what it was like to walk by faith together. They loved us like their own family. Some of those families from our dear first church have even refused to let miles or time separate our paths. They have prayed for us and supported us all of these years. Until they were grown, every year at Christmas our girls would receive a special Christmas ornament from one sweet family. Our tree gives witness to the undying love and the forever fellowship we have in the family of God.

We have had so many precious people invest in our lives that we dare not let our walk go without a testimony to God's faithfulness: God has and God will provide. We left our first church to go to a mission church in Indiana. We came there with little to nothing, but watched God provide. One sweet family from the mission purchased our appliances, as well as furnished the home we rented with amazing furniture purchased from local yard sales. We had people from church to church provide for us—from helping us with cars to hand-stitched keepsakes. As God has guided us, he has provided through his people, and these people have become like family. Dear reader, we miss a lot when we don't walk by faith. Faith walking makes us depend on God and one another. It binds our hearts together in love. As a matter of fact, walking by faith is the only way we can walk with God. However, once we step into the unknown, God brings amazing things to pass. As we meet one another's spiritual and physical needs, relationships are born and woven together for eternity. Our hearts are tightly bound by faith and our spirits encouraged. We are renewed with strength to keep walking with God.

Not only have we had God meet our needs through His people, but we have also seen God move through everyday circumstances. Once when our girls were young, my husband asked me to pray earnestly for

God to somehow provide us with money to pay our girl's monthly school payment. Billy was pastor of a small church congregation. Money was tight, but we desperately wanted to keep our girls in Christian school. I prayed as I went to drop them off at school that morning. On the way back home, a fellow pulled up beside me in the passing lane and motioned for me to pull over. As I wondered what could be wrong, I pulled to a nearby shoulder of the road. I rolled down my car window and, before I could reason it all out, this gentleman said, *"I want to buy your car."* Billy had purchased this car at a good price and done a wonderful job at cleaning it up. We had a FOR SALE sign in the back of this second vehicle for some time, but that day, God sent the right person at the right time to want that car immediately. We had kept praying until the answer came. I went from concerned about how we would have enough to praising God for the extra in the matter of an hour. When we go out obediently, we can watch him care for our every need. To go out empty and depend on God requires waiting. Seeing God work is exciting, and it will happen if we only put off the shoes of sight and put on the walking shoes of faith.

Could you testify of a provision in the time of faith? If so, describe it below.

_____

_____

_____

_____

When you walk by faith and not by sight, you will come to the point where asking God for detailed needs is a common practice and seeing him answer is a regular occurrence. You will be content with what you have because you know your treasure is not here below, and whatever God provides, new or used, will work fine. We have seen God meet not only our needs, but surprise us with our desires at times as well. One couple provided us with Bible-conference weekends and even a trip to Israel. It was Amazing!!! My study of the Bible has gone to new heights because of loving, obedient brothers and sisters in Christ. Another dear couple continues to uphold us with loving support and prayer. Every time we see them, they bless us. (I dare not mention their names, they wouldn't have it. That is just the kind of loving folks you meet on the journey of faith.) Sweet brothers and sisters in Christ have provided us with quilts, places to stay, loving gifts, constant prayer and loving support. When Billy was serving as an interim pastor, one family cooked us the most amazing home-cooked meals every Sunday for two years, as well as typed the book you now hold in your hand (talk about treating you like family). It makes you more thankful when you know that these gifts are perfect gifts from God. When you know that you did not obtain them yourself. You must give him the glory. Not that we don't work hard and "earn our keep" where he has called us, we should do all as unto God. Yet, when so much of our time is given to his service, he will provide scrip, purse, bread, and clothes. It keeps your faith exercised when you go to him for every need, and it makes you appreciate the answer. God provides every piece of bread, every word you need to say, the money you need, the clothes you need, and the strength to walk in faith (Isaiah 40:31). Wait on God and watch Him answer. Remember how God provided manna in the wilderness; then the quail and water as well. Don't forget his wonders that he performed before his disciples. Fish and bread from a lad's lunch fed thousands, money from a fish's mouth paid taxes. He will do the same for you, but it first requires removing those shoes of sight. Go ahead and put on your walking shoes of faith and take up the staff of God's Word—they are all you will need. Walking by faith is challenging, yet walking by faith is also exciting!

# Day Three

## Shake Off the Dust
## Faith Endures Suffering

After telling his disciples not to be concerned with the details of the journey, Jesus told them how to handle rejection. "Shake off the dust," he said.

Write out Luke 9:5

_____

_____

_____

_____

_____

We read in this passage that the dust _____ against those that do not heed the gospel.

I hope you wrote <u>testifies</u> in the blank? Now let's think. How could dust particles give a testimony? In considering this question for myself, I couldn't help but wonder if this might involve the dust being one day used as forensic evidence—could be. If a rock has the capacity to cry out, dust certainly could testify. It happens everyday in the courts of our lands. Dust, blood, hair, skin cells, individual DNA—all of these testify in courts. We read in several passages about the blood crying out against the guilty murderers such as Cain (Gen. 4:10). Won't it be incredibly breathtaking in the great court of Heaven when the forensics are there and used as testimony and proof that the gospel was proclaimed, yet rejected?

It is discouraging to be rejected. Sometimes we feel like we are seldom heard. We visit and share the gospel time after time, and place after place with many apathetic refusals. We grow heavy with burdens when we see the conditions of lost friends and loved ones. Our hearts groan with grief at the desire for them to experience the joy and compassion we know. When we see such need and we have such riches, it hurts to realize they are too hardened to receive such a wonderful and eternal treasure; it weighs heavy. However, when we have been obedient to God's leading and shared time and again what He has told us to share, then we leave it on their own ground. As sand that clung to the sandal of the ancient traveler, we must shake it off before the Lord, and then we must walk on.

Jesus was perfect in every way, and he had rejections. That's due to the fact that true love gives a choice. The rich young ruler went away sad after being told exactly what held him back from surrender (Mark 10:21). Jesus wept over Jerusalem when she would not come to him for comfort (Luke 19:41). Our Savior knows all to well about the pain of rejection.

Dust will cling to you and bog you down. Dust can collect around your feet and irritate. Words that doubters speak, cruel accusations, mockings— all of these can cause discomfort, if we don't shake them off. The Israelites had their "dust." They walked through many desert places to conquer and to claim ground. The Jewish believers had to shake the Canaanites from their feet more than once. Paul was also reminded in Acts to shake the dust of rejection from his soul-winning sandals. We too must shake off the dust during the journey or we will get bogged down in the mud on enemy turf (Mt.10:14).

Remember we are only passing through. We are ambassadors with a message. We have the word of God. However, only a few will really accept it. We need not be surprised when we are ridiculed or persecuted. It's part of the true walk of faith. Jesus promised we would suffer persecution. "All those who live righteous in Christ Jesus will suffer persecution" (II Timothy 3:12). As a matter of fact, we should be more concerned if we are not at times despised and rejected of men. Jesus said we would be sent out as lambs among wolves, but he promised He would be with us. He told us to take up our cross daily and follow him (Luke 14:27). A cross is a place where you are displayed, humiliated and hurt, yet it has another side to it. Jesus shook off death, and he cast his shoe over sin. (Casting a shoe is a sign of conquering or being against something (Ps. 60:8). On the other side of the cross was the crown. We are as he—a pilgrim on a journey. This world is not our home, it is the valley of death we pass through (Psalms 23). We must shake off the dust in order to travel with him and continue our walk. The faithful pilgrim shakes off a lot of dust and keeps on walking. In order to walk with God, we must die to self-concerns and be set apart for selfless serving.

We see in the life of our Lord that true serving is selfless serving. He came to a world that had no room for him, he lived a sojourner's life, and he died as a criminal. Jesus more than understands our sorrows and rejections. We've seen him shake a lot of dust from his feet, yet we never saw him quit. We must go on, brother and sister. Our time is short and our message is vital. Our eternity is secured, but many are desperately looking for the truth we have. Is our comfort and acceptance so important on this earth? Be encouraged that it is only a journey. This world is not your final destination. You carry a cross now, but you will soon cast it off as a shoe. You are on your way to a crown. Our ways are foolish to the world and becoming more and more unaccepted. Attempts are made to silence our beliefs, but man can never silence the untouchable spirit and soul. Here we are "booed" and sent away, yet from Heaven we are cheered and welcomed. Pilgrims on a journey, that's what we are. Remember, you are an ambassador with a message.

In closing, Billy and I have had our share of naysayers and dusty doubters. He, being a minister of the gospel, has to stay in the practice of being a "shoe shaker." And I, being a pastor's wife have to resist the temptation "to cast a shoe". (Ha, Ha) We have had the mudslingers throw what they could. I could share many an example, but since that dust has been shaken off behind us, I don't think I will go back to collect dirt. Anyway, our job is to wash feet and not keep track of the muddy prints, right? Following Jesus is not easy, but it is the most rewarding life one could imagine. Walking the missionary trail gets very dusty. Yet faith is where we keep the leather to the path and shake off the dust because faith endures suffering.

# Day Four

## Faith serves:
## Washing feet

"If I then, your Lord and Master, have washed your feet; ye also ought to wash one another's feet. For I have given you an example, that ye should do as I have done to you." John 13:14-15

More amazing to me than the ability to shake off dust is the fact that Jesus washed the dust from the feet of self-centered men. He even stooped humbly to serve the one who would betray him. Can you imagine the example given by our Savior? Doesn't it astonish you that God humbled himself to the point of serving the one who would help plot his death? He took a basin and towel, and he washed the feet of Judas. I will never cease to live in wonder at how Jesus perfectly practiced what he taught. Our humble God knelt before sinful humans. Instead of a celebration over all Jesus had done or attention to what was to come for him, the disciples turned inward. Judas betrayed him, Thomas doubted him, Peter denied him, and James and John strove to see who would be seated next to him. All of this happened as Jesus was communicating to them his soon-coming death. Their fleshly aspirations were exalted as his plans of sacrifice were humbly spoken. You see, faith not only endures rejection, faith serves the oppressor; it washes feet. The one walking in the shoes of faith moves on from shaking off the dust of rejecters to washing the feet of the doubters. Why? Because faith is forgiving, and true faith always serves.

Washing feet is part of our calling. Now, hold on, readers, I'm not expecting you to find the basin and the towel and start asking for shoes. That was an ancient physical need due to the dusty walks of the desert. In the day we live in, "washing feet" is a spiritual task. Jesus' example was calling us to a greater service than literally washing feet. We are to take up the water of the Word of God and encourage our brothers and sisters in Christ. We practice what we profess when we go to one with selfish grim and help to clear the "dirt" from their "feet." Maybe they are cast down and we share a promise—a promise from God's Word that will wash the doubt away. Maybe they have thrown dirt on us and are covered in it themselves. Could we not go and wash their feet? To "wash their feet" could be a simple act of love, a simple service that could brighten their day, a card, a visit, a gift, a continual friendship, a meal, or a secret act of service. It could even mean helping someone we dislike with a difficult task. To bear another's burdens is to wash their feet. We all need it. Our feet make contact with this corrupt world everyday. We constantly walk on the dust, and we need living water to cleanse the filth. God needs those who will take up the basin and towel and wash feet.

Have you washed anyone's feet today? I've just had mine washed. As I was busy about editing this manuscript, I heard a knock at our door. I opened the door to find a beautiful unexpected gift from the florist. Two ladies from our church sent flowers, white Christmas poinsettias, to us. The tag read "To our Pastor and Family". I am wiping away tears as I am amazed at how God works through His sweet servants to encourage our family. These two ladies are widows, and by their act of kindness, they washed my feet today. I have felt overwhelmed the last few days with loads of work, and concerned for family members. I told no one but my husband. However, God knew, and at just the right time He presented me with a cheery gift of encouragement. I was presented with the picture of how these ladies have had disappointments, yet chose to live on with cheer and thoughtfulness. Those flowers were a source of a heavenly foot washing. It's nice to have the water of love washing over you when you have the weight of heavy, dusty burdens on your feet.

Janet Hagen is another mighty "foot washer" for God. She, another triumphant widow, leads our Women's Missionary Union meetings at our church. Many ladies have their feet washed (spiritually speaking) by these weekly fellowships and Janet's sense of humor. She has put aside her widowhood of grieving to wash feet. Not long ago, during a meeting while we worked to make gospel dolls for missionaries, pillow cases for those in the hospital, and baby blankets for newborns, we had a special experience. As we were busy about our "makings", one of the ladies of our church asked us come to the kitchen one at a time. She sent for us and said she had something special she felt led to do. When it came my time, I walked into the room and closed the door as instructed. Mrs. Muriel Barnhill, a sweet woman of God took my hands, washed them in a bowl, and prayed over them as she washed and dried my hands. She continued to pray as she finished, by covering them with lotion. How humbled I was. No doubt she had been thinking of us before our meeting that day. By her humble service, we were assured of her love and felt her desire to renew us. I can only imagine the shock and awe that came across the followers of Jesus as he took the basin and towel and began to wash his disciple's feet. I wonder if he conducted a prayer washing for his disciples, as Mrs. Muriel had done for us. They did have some dirt which needed to be washed away.

What kind of attitudes needed to be washed from the disciples minds? Share your answer here:

_____

_____

_____

_____

I don't know about you, but I saw some grime of self-centeredness on James' and John's feet. How about Peter, did you notice those dark brown patches of impulsive tendencies and "save self image" clumps that he treaded in? Thomas's feet appeared clean at first, but as the shoes came off, it was obvious the mud of doubt had caked under the bottom of his arch. Come to think about it, I'm sure I even saw him limping on his way in. And then, in spite of everything, Judas comes in for the Lord's Supper filthy from head to toe. He is not clean at all!

Take a moment to read John 13:10-15.

Write out any thoughts that stood out to you. _____

_____

_____

I hope these truths are coming alive in your own heart as they have in mine. I see myself before Jesus just as the disciples: a believer who remains much in need of daily spiritual foot washings as long as I remain in this dusty world. Not only do we as Christians need the fresh water of the Word, encouragement, and love each day, but Jesus points out in John 13:14 that we also need to wash one another's feet.

Some of the churches in our town of Corbin, Ky., participate in an annual "Love Loud" community event. Churches in our area come together and "love loudly" by joining in a team effort to reach out and serve the surrounding area. It's a citywide spiritual foot washing of sorts—isn't that neat! This is our first year to participate, and it has been quite an experience. We all met a few days ago wearing our green-themed t-shirts and went out to purchase canned goods and dry foods for our event. Our girls were all able to participate as well, so it was a fun family event. It was beautiful! Green t-shirts were everywhere around our local store. It was also a time of sweet fellowship. Christians greeted one another with happy smiles. We were on the same mission and shared the same life-changing salvation and love. During this weeklong event of preparation and service, we have the opportunity to offer random acts of service to elderly people, mothers, families, and individuals who need the discomfort of loneliness washed away. Some go to the laundry mat with rolls of quarters then proceed to wash, dry, and fold for anyone needing help. Others head to the local gas pumps filling up tanks for anyone open to receive free gas. The usual question that follows is: *"Why are you doing this?"* You see, "washing feet" has a way of getting one's attention.

Let's close today's study in a joint prayer.

*Dear Father,*

*Thank you for all the times you washed our feet. Sometimes through an encouraging word; other times by way of a scripture in a note or a card. Through songs, sermons, Sunday school teachers, and many other acts of kindness, you gently wash us and pray for our well being. Help us as your church, your body of believers, to go out as you have instructed us and wash one another's feet today.*

*In the precious name of Jesus, the most humble servant,*
*Amen*

# Day Five

## Walking with God:
## Faith Walks Humbly

L ast, but not least, walking shoes are made for walking. We choose good, sturdy shoes of endurance to withstand the wear and tear of countless steps and various terrains. The best quality leather is chosen, and consideration is given to every detail. For the Christian, the badger-skin shoes of faith are the best. These waterproof, tough and proven, and time-tested shoes will not disappoint the traveler.

Dr. M.R. DeHaan shares interesting research on the leather used for shoes during Bible times: "These badgers' skins had no colorful beauty; they were drab, dull, and bluish grey." He goes on to relate the badgers' skins to the deity of Jesus. While the outside of the badger's skin covering was nothing appealing to the eye, what it veiled inside was beautiful (Isaiah 53:2-3). He also connects Christ' fleshly covering to the tabernacle: "The badgers' skins, then, represent all that the world can see in the person of the Lord Jesus Christ, until they have been born again. They are still on the outside where the winds tear, the rain pelts, the sun bakes, and the frost bites. It is the exposed portion of the tabernacle that they are able to see," says DeHaan.[4] The badger's skin was used in the tabernacle. It was the outer covering that withstood the harsh elements and veiled the inner beauty of the temple. Christ's body withstood the terrible treatments of the cross, but all who are in Christ know He is full of beauty. Our badger's skin shoes of faith are carefully pieced and crafted by the master cobbler. We have available shoes made to tread over any path of this world. We must have these sturdy shoes in our Christian life for our walk of faith.

Consider how important walking is: Walking strengthens muscles and increases circulation. Doctors highly recommend it. God designed it, and we need it. Walking allows us to travel at a slower pace and witness God's creation as we go. In Bible times, walking was a natural part of each day. Why did so many people walk instead of travel by horse, camel, or donkey? We are not sure, but possibly due to the fact that other modes of transportation were costly. We know that kings and leaders traveled by horse and camels. A humble king even chose to ride a donkey during times of special celebrations and coronations out of pure desire to meet the people on their level. He wanted to serve. Maybe walking was a sign of a patient man as well. Could it be that a patient man chose to walk? Walking does reflect humility. When Jesus called his disciples, he called them to follow Him. To follow someone is to walk with them. God calls man to walk with Him. Many times in scripture our relationship with God is described as walking with God.

Consider how our Creator designed us. We can learn a lot from how God designed our literal physical ability to walk. With two feet to hold up our being, we are reminded that we walk in pairs such as: Truth and Love, Joy and Peace, Contentment and Patience. The feet are located at the base of our being to remind us that our walk is to be humble. Then, too, God gave us ten toes. I personally think this was to emphasize the fact that we are to walk in His ten commands. Isn't that amazing? We must walk with Him in order to keep these ten. We cannot keep them apart from Him, but with His strength, we can walk in them. What exactly does it mean to walk with God? In our spiritual journey with our Savior, walking means that our thoughts, convictions, and deeds are in line with God's Word, God's commands, and God's will. Our walk with God is a relationship with God. It is not following a program but a person. It is not an empty religion of rules; it is an active relationship with the person of Jesus Christ. He is real, and He lives. He comes to reside inside the heart and mind of everyone who invites Him into their lives. Micah 6:8 tells us that God requires us to walk humbly with him. God's word tells us for two to walk together, they must agree. That's where the humbly walking part comes into play. Faith calls upon God to lead and faith follows unseen and in total trust; faith follows. In Psalms 25:1-5, the psalmist pleads with God to guide and lead him into the right way. We, too, need to cry out for God's guidance as we, like those of scripture, have been called to follow Him.

Surely, you have witnessed those who have walked humbly before God in your lifetime. List some of those precious saints here in their honor, and perhaps add a short word about their humble walk.

_____

_____

_____

_____

Walking with God requires walking in His Spirit. The powerful fruit of the Spirit is required to walk by faith, and the shoes of faith are the only kind that can make the journey. Made to travel over rugged terrain and to endure mountainous climbs, shoes of faith can protect us and enable us to walk in the Spirit of God. Making the exchange from sight to faith covers us with peace, joy, love, longsuffering, and gentleness. We rest in the fact that God's word is the only staff we need and that our steps are protected by his promises. With staff in hand and sandals strapped securely, we can walk in the walking shoes of faith step by step.

## Step By Step

He does not lead me year by year
Nor even day by day
But step by step my path unfolds;
My Lord directs my way.

Tomorrow's paths I do not know,
I only know this minute;
But He will say, "This is the way,
By faith now walk ye in it."

And I am glad that it is so.
Today is enough to bear;
And when tomorrow comes, His grace
Shall far exceed its care

What need to worry then, or fret?
The God who gave His Son
Holds all my moments in His hand
And gives them one by one.

-Barbara C. Ryberg

# WEEK SIX

## Shoes of Mercy

# Day One

# The Straying Prodigal

"But the father said to his servants, Bring forth the best robe,
and put it on him; and put a ring of his hand, and shoes on his feet."

Luke 15:22

Realizing that God will take care of all needs throughout our
Christian journey helps us to turn our attention to the care
of others. When we follow God by faith, we will stop with
Him along the way to help those in need. The straying prodigal and the
pleading poor wait for us to hear their cry and to have compassion on
them. The paralyzed sinner and the persecuted weak need us to bring
the glorious hope of the Word of God to their desperate state and see
them through to freedom.

We read in Luke 15:22 that the father in this story is very
interested in helping the prodigal to be restored. Notice that the
prodigal had lost his robe, his ring of identity, and finally his shoes. He
needed love. The question then comes to us: Will we stop with Jesus to
help the prodigal put on his shoes of identity? Will we share with the
poor, go to the lost, and speak for the persecuted? They need covering;
their feet are hurting.

We are to respond to the straying prodigal with love when he returns home. Our response is to be that of the servant in Luke 15:22. We are to bring shoes and put them on his feet. It's not always an easy task. The feet of the prodigal will be very dusty; they will need to be washed (maybe several times). Then they will need someone to walk with them. We usually prefer to walk with those who are of similar stride, do we not? However, the Christian walking in a heavenly gate will be willing to slow down to encourage those behind him who have lost their way. Sometimes it is very uncomfortable to comfort the prodigal. We have a choice to make. Will we look down on the one gone astray, like the elder brother of Luke 15, or will we take the role of the servant and obey our master as he says, bring "shoes for his feet"?

For today's study, read Luke 15. After reading this chapter, I want you to consider the prodigal's return from the servant's perspective. Especially the one who may have washed the prodigal son's feet on the day he finally returned.

Record your thoughts on what the servant might have experienced. (What emotions might he have felt?)

_____

_____

_____

_____

The task of caring for the shoes and feet of others was nothing new for the servant. As each family member or visitor came into the house, their feet were burdened and dusty, but the servant took care of them. He removed the sandals and bore the dusty leathers on his arm. Then he washed the feet of the individual and thus showed them respect. It was a daily task, but I somehow feel the washing of the prodigal son's feet was a special occurrence. I wonder, was the water in the basin mixed with tears from the eyes of the servant that washed the prodigal's feet? Did the servant experience tender emotion as he shod the prodigal with new sandals? Was this a monumental occasion for the servant?

Yes, chances are that this event of service to the prodigal son was one not to be forgotten, especially for the man of service. Can you imagine the stench and filth that the prodigal brought with him? Fresh out of the hog pen! (How is that for an oxymoron?) The prodigal was rugged, dirty, and very unpleasant to see or smell, yet the father made sure that his son was welcomed back with royal treatment. Maybe the father's mind was drawn back to a time when his son was a young boy and had come home dirty and unkempt. This was still his boy. The father wasted no time, he didn't have to lecture or nag, his son had come home with repentance. The prodigal confessed *"Father, I have sinned against heaven, and in thy sight, and am no more worthy to be called thy son"* (Luke 15:21). However, be sure to note that even before the repentance, and before the younger son spoke a word, the father ran to his son and kissed him. He had been looking for him every day! What compassion this parent had for his child. The father instructed the servant to bring a ring of identity and put it on his son's finger, as well as the best robe, prime rib, and yes, shoes for his feet. That's our lesson in dealing with the prodigal—when he comes home, exchange dust for divine. Give him shoes for his feet, and maybe even … share your own shoes.

Have you ever gone on an extended outing with your children and advised them several times beforehand to wear comfortable shoes? No flip-flops! No shoes that would wear a blister! Wear comfortable shoes you would say, right? However, I'm sure you responded as I when your child came to you in misery and asked to exchange shoes for just a while. You had mercy on their poor feet and you walked in their shoes, and they walked in yours while they received comfort and you took on their pain. Jesus surely did that for us, and we must do the same for the prodigal. Welcome him and her back with shoes for their feet. Our Lord reshod Peter after his denial, and Peter went on to give us encouraging words in his biblical text about holding on through terrible times. John Mark was covered to walk again after quitting on the missionary journeys of Paul, and we have his testimonies of God's faithfulness in his records in the gospel book of Mark. The prodigal needs to be comforted with the gospel shoes of peace.

Somewhere along the road, the prodigal took a wrong turn. Convinced it was a better path, he followed the sign that was labeled

"Alternate Route to Happiness—Turn Here." Time after time he had the feeling to turn back; yet self-reasoning convinced him to travel this way a little longer. Finally, realizing he was desperate, he had the deepest desire to go home. As the prodigal son stood in the filth of the unclean, he hit rock bottom. Even as a boy, he had been taught about God's ways. He had known of holiness and uncleanness. Never did he go near a pigpen, let alone consider eating alongside these animals known to be unclean by his people. Isn't that just where sin leads the one who strays—desperate, shamed, guilty, and no longer feeling worthy? Yes, the enemy keeps the prodigal at bay and estranged from home. "You are not worthy to return!" he shouts to the straying prodigal. Desolate, disgraced, and guilty, that's where the wrong turn leads the prodigal. They allow the enemy of their souls to detour them to the ways of death. Death of dignity, joy, and peace is always his goal.

My friend, Melissa, shared a neat illustration with me about how easy it is to get "stuck in the mud."

### *The Rubber Boots*

*As kids, my cousins and I loved running and playing outside. I was the only girl but I could play in the dirt and catch frogs and snakes with the best of them. My aunt and uncle owned a 35-acre farm and we had a lot of fun playing in the fields and hiking through the woods. We were always full of energy and constantly looking for more adventures to get into—or mischief, as our parents would call it. Our parents bought each of us a pair of tall rubber boots because they were tired of us messing up our good school shoes with our adventurous excursions. These boots came up to our knees and we felt as if they would shield us from anything. At the time, I was nine years old. My younger cousin, Kevin, was six and my older cousin, Brad, was ten.*

*On this particular day, we each put on our big rubber boots and went outside to test them out. It had been raining the day before and there was a lot of soft mud on the tree farm. With these boots, we felt like we could do anything and not get dirty. We found every mud hole and puddle that we could find and jumped and splashed into them. As I approached a mud puddle that hadn't yet been investigated, I jumped right in. This was much more than a mud puddle; this mud was quite deep! I was excited about the discovery! "Hey, I found some deep, deep mud over here!" My cousins came in and immediately jumped in, too. It was a thick mud and as I stepped through, it came almost to the top of my boots. At first it was great fun, at least until I tried to get out of the hole. I tried to get my feet out and they wouldn't budge. My cousins were still near the edge so they were able to get out. Brad came closer to me to help me get out and quickly found that he was stuck as well. Kevin decided that the best idea was to get his little red wagon and try to pull us out. I am sure to the outside viewer this would have been a hilarious sight! My older cousin grabbed on to the wagon and managed to get free from the mud. My boots, however, were not going anywhere. As my cousins pulled me with the little red wagon, one of my feet came out of the boot so I decided to go ahead and pull the other one out, too. I was free but the boots were left behind in the sludge.*

*The driveway that we crossed was graveled with sharp lava rock and was quite painful on my bare feet as we made our way back to the house. When we came into the house, our parents just looked at us in total disbelief! Our fathers were a little perturbed, as we were covered from head to toe with mud. Our moms laughed hysterically! We looked ridiculous and it reminded them of the silly things that they did as kids. There was not any harm done. They sent us to clean up and all was well. As for the boots, they were recovered the next day, but not without the help of my uncles' backhoe.*

*It's so funny how we thought those rubber boots would protect us from all of the dirt and mud. I got stuck in the mess in spite of the "magical" protection of tall rubber boots. Even with my cousin's great intention of getting me out of the mess, he just sunk right into the same mess that I was in. It's much easier to get pulled into a quagmire than to be pulled out of one.* -Melissa Walker

Proverbs 14:12 tells *us, "There is a way which seemeth right unto a man, but the end thereof are the ways of death."*

There will be many prodigals who continue on their path of straying, yet for those who come home, we need to take out the basin and the towel and be as a good servant who rejoices with the father by restoring the prodigal. We need to clean and cover not drag and nag. The prodi-"gal" has enough mud on her feet. Her wounds are already evident. She needs no more mud and no more wounds. What she needs is the balm of Gilead and good coverings for her feet. Our Christian sisters need encouraging. They need to be restored to a right standing. How amazing is the timing of our Lord! As I sat typing this section of today's study, an announcement came over the Christian radio station that illustrates today's focus. The lady on the radio was informing the listening audience of a weekly prayer ministry themed "Praying the Prodigal Home." This church has the idea. When the prodigal is away, they need prayer, and when they return home, they need shoes of mercy.

What do the shoes of mercy look like? Well, for starters, they are not the secondhand shoes that are given just to justify contributing to cause. Such shoes would be a shameful gift. They bear worn-out holes of judgment and stains of intolerance. The returning prodigal has no need for shoes of mockery or belittlement. Neither does the prodigal desire to wear the shoes of slavery or scorn. No need of legalistic shoes from the Pharisee cobblers—woven with pride and ridicule. Sandals of security, that's what the prodigal needs. These shoes are lined with soft crimson on the inside and beaming with royalty on the outside. Beautiful shoes that are adorned with jewels of great price are to be given to the prodigal who has come home.

Song of Solomon 7:1 describes the scene. *"How beautiful are thy feet with shoes, O prince's daughter!"*

# Day Two

## Shoes for the Needy

Galatians 6:2 "Bear ye one another's burdens,
And so fulfill the law of Christ."

It was one of those times that I could have laid down on the floor and wept. The glass window on the floor below our feet displayed an encased pile of shoes. Some belonging to children, some belonging to adults, the actual shoes of Holocaust victims lay before my eyes. The shoes of these helpless victims gave visual evidence to the lives thrown away. Due to man's wicked pride and desired power, these poor were sold for "a pair of shoes" and trampled underfoot. Hitler was a prime example of one who walked over ones he esteemed poor and unworthy, and the charred remains of Jewish shoes bore the sad story.

Amos 2:6 "Thus saith the Lord; for three transgressions of Israel, and for four, I will not turn away the punishment thereof; because they sold the righteous for silver, and the poor for a pair of shoes."

My heart broke in that Israeli museum as I imagined the feet that once walked in those shoes. Satan has no thought for the pitiful, no mercy for the young or old, and no compassion for the needy. The enemy knows that the poor are near to the heart of God; therefore Satan targets those weak and favored ones. Their torment is his objective. However, God has commanded His people to provide for the poor and to protect them. With compassion, we are to reach out to the poor in our "gates"—our town. To harden our hearts and close our hands is to greatly offend Almighty God.

Let's consider the poor. Who were they in Jesus' day and time?

Describe your picture of the "poor" in Jesus' day.

_____

_____

_____

_____

Now, compare it to the needy of our day. How would you describe them?

_____

_____

_____

_____

Were your answers similar? Mine were.

Let's move on now to discuss the difference between the poor and the sluggard. Note that there is a vast difference between a sluggard and those with sincere need. It is an affront to God to enable a lazy person. Paul instructs us in II Thessalonians 3:10 that an idle person is either to work or not to eat. Work is a blessed gift of God that we as humans need. It was ordained before sin, and it is good. God blesses hard work but frowns on those who waste their days in idleness.

Underline Proverbs 6:6 in your Bible. God gives us an illustration there in Proverbs 6 on how He expects us to work. Although we know that God has a work for every person, those who are: orphaned and too young to provide, widowed with no children to provide, sick beyond mobility, or a strangers who cannot find work need us to help carry their burden until they can find employment. The ones imprisoned to greed need to learn the wisdom to work over the desire to take. Those who can work should work, with all their might as unto the Lord (Col. 3:23). We are not to encourage or enable laziness, but instead we are to help ones addicted to taking learn the gift of responsibility. The Bible clears up the difference between those who *act* needy and those who *are* needy.

God's word stresses over and over the groups that define His burden. The lonely widow, the desperate orphan, the cast aside stranger, the weak, and needy—these are the poor. The poor are the ones without provision or protection. They are vulnerable. The sweet widow needs shoes of mercy. The orphaned child needs love and shelter. The stranger needs security and kindness. The imprisoned soul needs to be visited. Each person needs to know they have meaning and purpose. It is our job to be the hands and feet of Jesus and to show them that they matter to God and to us.

Kendra Petrey knows how it feels to be taken in and shod with shoes of love and mercy. Her story is a beautiful one, which I would like to share with you.

## Kendra's Story

"I was born in Seoul, South Korea on September 23, 1985. For the first eighteen months of my life, I lived in an orphanage. I was able to talk, but for some unknown reason, I never walked. I think the orphanage was so crowded that they maybe didn't have enough time for another pair of feet. To make a long story short, I was adopted by the two greatest parents, Audrey and Kathy Petrey. They had to teach me to talk in English. Then in my new home, I learned to walk. I recently graduated from Eastern Kentucky University and I have a job. If it weren't for my parents praying and asking God for guidance, I don't know that I could have done any of this, or even walked. Because of my parents and God, I was not only able to take my first step physically, but also my first step toward a wonderful salvation in Jesus Christ. To this day, I thank and praise God Almighty for saving me and for giving me a blessing in the form of godly parents. I thank him for the ability to do everyday things." — Kendra Petrey

Aubra and Kathy not only provided shoes of mercy, they also taught Kendra how to walk—"an everyday thing" as she thankfully expressed. I am blessed to know Kendra. She has such a beautiful heart for God. As she has been richly graced with the mercy of God, she in return wears the shoes of mercy quite beautifully in serving others. She was a part of my young ladies' Sunday school class when this shoe study was but an exciting thought. Her parents, Aubra and Kathy, are humble servants. They have lovingly worked for years in the children's ministry at the West Corbin Baptist Church. Spiritually speaking, they have taken in many and helped them learn to walk with God. I am amazed by those like this family who wear the shoes of mercy so well.

Who is it around us that we can take in and share our bountiful blessings with? Maybe it is one or two of the bus children at church who are like spiritual orphans. How about one of our widows that sit home alone and marks on her calendar, "Nobody came today"? Jesus would meet their need. Will we? Will we go to the ones in prison and treat them with love and compassion? God cares for the weak, and we have a great responsibility to show them mercy.

We finish out today's study a little differently. I'm letting you out early to get started on a little … homework.

First, I will ask you today to take some time to educate yourself on how your church ministers to the needy around your community. Are you aware of how much effort is given by your church to reach out to the elderly, sick, imprisoned, and fatherless? Ask your leaders about this, then get involved. God wants His main priorities to be ours as well.

Next, let's go a little closer to home. Take some time to consider what we do as a family to reach out to the unprotected, uncovered, and unloved.

Finally, what will we do as an individual today to help a widow, orphan, or imprisoned soul? Take some time to pray over this, asking God to reveal needs around you.

# Day Three

## Paralyzed Feet

"How can they call on him in whom they have not believed? And how shall they believe on him of whom they have not heard? And how shall they hear without a preacher? And how shall they preach, except they be sent? As it is written, how beautiful are the feet of them that preach the gospel of peace, and bring glad tidings of good things."
Romans 10: 14-15

In the last chapter, "Walking Shoes," we looked at the missionary's journey. We saw in that lesson how to go—by faith; yet, to whom do we go? Matthew 28:19-20 tells us to go into "all" the world with the gospel of Christ. As we just read, they cannot come to us, so we must go to them. They are paralyzed by sin, rendering them unable to come—powerless to walk to Christ. They are lame and blind. Knowing this, Jesus always went to the sinner. He searched them out in many different places—by a well, up a tree, lying pitifully on the roadside begging. Jesus went to them, and when He found them, He didn't just put shoes on their feet, He restored limbs! He healed them to walk eternally. We, too, must realize that those without Christ are paralyzed. They do not come to church for they are bound by Satan's blinders, and they are maimed by his deceitful lies. They lay calling for help, "Someone, please bring me water," "Bring me healing," "Someone, please help me to walk." We must hear their cries and learn a lesson from our Lord, Jesus, the living water, came to them. Knowing they would not come, he had compassion on their thirsty state and came to them. We as Christians must change our focus from improving programs inside the church, and instead be aware that we must take the living water to those who are lost and paralyzed by sin.

Let's go to Acts 3:1-10 for our study today. After reading this passage, answer the following questions:

What did the man in these scriptures suffer from?

_____

_____

How long had he been dealing with this problem?

_____

Now, look at Mark 5:1-15.

How was this man "paralyzed"?

Why couldn't he get help?

_____

_____

How does this account relate to those who are paralyzed by sin?

_____

_____

How wonderful! When he could not help himself, Jesus came to him. Isn't that what we are to do as the body of Christ? Most certainly, we are to take Jesus to them, and take them to Jesus. There is a wonderful illustration of this in Mark 2:1-12.

Look at Mark 2:1-12.
Note the difficulty of the task in this passage. Study these verses and then write three facts about the determination of the friends.

1. _____

_____

2. _____

_____

3. _____

_____

Did you see that they were willing to do the following?
- find a way (when there seemed to be no way)
- do something different
- take a risk

Can you imagine the distraction in the house when the patchwork began to crumble from the roof above? That had to be a sermon stopper. As a pastor's daughter and pastor's wife, I've seen a few odd distractions during some services. I can remember once a dog coming down the aisle during a summer service. On another occasion, a drunken fellow came in looking for his wife. (That was a bit dramatic.) Yet, probably to top them all, I once witnessed a minister's false teeth fly forth right out of his mouth. In the middle of a strong sermon, he gathered a breath to restate his point, and out they flew. I was sitting up front and got an eyewitness account. Not to worry, though: He caught them in mid-flight, put them in his suit pocket, mentioned something about how the enemy wasn't going to stop him, and kept right on with his sermon. What a preacher!

As we know, Jesus was not taken by surprise when He was interrupted; he welcomed the steps of faith, which I am sure only emphasized the sermon. There is nothing like having a living demonstration to make a point. Right in the middle of His sermon Jesus receives the one coming from the rooftop and heals him right there before everyone's eyes. We don't have to wonder what their dinner conversation involved. "What a sermon!" was probably one of many comments. No doubt the people of that house congregation came face to face with the need of the paralyzed.

If we look closely, we will see them too. The pleading people paralyzed by sin are all around us. As we walk closely with God, we will not just see them, but we will feel a burden for their lost state. Our hearts will drive our feet to go to them, our compassion will compel our hands to reach out to them, and the burning truth of the gospel in our soul will burst forth to give light to their darkness. If we allow the mighty power of God's truth to proceed from our hearts, we will see their powerless feet and their paralyzed person rise up to walk in the shoes of mercy.

# Day Four

## Persecuted Feet

Luke 10:27-34

[27]"And he answering said, Thou shalt love the Lord thy God with all thy heart, and with all thy soul, and with all thy strength, and with all thy mind; and thy neighbor as thyself.

[28] And he said unto him, Thou hast answered right: this do and thou shalt live.

[29]But he, willing to justify himself, said unto Jesus, and who is my neighbor?

[30] And Jesus answering said, A certain man went down from Jerusalem to Jericho, and fell among thieves, which stripped him of his raiment, and wounded him, and departed, leaving him half dead.

[31]And by chance there came down a certain priest that way: and when he saw him, he passed by on the other side.

[32] And likewise a Levite, when he was at the place, came and looked on him, and passed by on the other side.

[33]But a certain Samaritan, as he journeyed, came where he was: and when he saw him, he had compassion on him,

[34]And went to him, and bound up his wounds, pouring in oil and wine, and set him on his own beast, and brought him to an inn, and took care of him."

Take a few moments to circle the acts of compassion that was kindly bestowed on the injured man in the previous reading.

Could the man pay him anything in return? _____

What drove this Samaritan to go the "extra" mile for this stranger?

_____

_____

_____

In our day, we want comfort. Consumed with our own pleasures and goals, we often have little thought or care for those who are hurting, just as the priest and the Levite passed by the persecuted man on the Jericho road. Many have little to do with the beaten and the bruised. Are we really willing to walk on the Jericho road, by the leprous colonies, or through the graveyards? Will we look with compassion upon the beaten and bloody, or will we step aside and look away? Do we go to those we can comfort or to those who will comfort us?

Many around us are hurting without anyone to plead their cause. From the unborn in the womb who have no voice in keeping their lives, to those who bravely put their lives on the line for their faith, many suffer at the hand of evil men who run to shed innocent blood. Maybe if we realized that our Christian responsibility is to find out who our neighbor is, and what our neighbor is experiencing, then we would be more prone to put on the surgeon's shoes of compassion.

Maybe too we would pray more if we understood that our prayers can cross the oceans of separation to persecuted feet around the world. If we educate ourselves to the suffering, we would pray more sacrificially. Surely if we but take the time to put a name and a face with the suffering, we would not forget them. Resources such as *Voice of the Martyrs* and *Daily Bread* give names of both victims and missionaries who desperately need our prayers. To ignore their cries is to bear guilt for their burdens. I wonder, do our churches take time to feel the pain of the persecuted? God cares about people everywhere. The feet of the church are suffering. Missionaries are giving their homes and lives, persecuted Christians are undergoing terror and torture, and right here at home in our states, babies are being slaughtered. Are we numb to the pain in the feet of our church body throughout the world? Are we going along like all is fine when a terrible leprous disease threatens the feet of the body of Christ, while we don't even feel the pain?

Brittani Graening felt the pain of her Haitian brothers and sisters. Years ago, upon hearing that Haiti had undergone a terrible earthquake, Brittani was brokenhearted. She had been in Haiti just one year prior to the earth-shattering quake. As she was there doing mission work, she had seen their faces, she had shared their joys, and she had felt their pain. While serving in Haiti, the children especially captured her heart. The boys and girls had surrounded her as she walked through the rough terrain. They removed the rocks out of her path so she wouldn't stumble. These young strangers were showing such love. Her heart was wrapped with affection for these ones that she had come to help. You know, if you have ever been on a mission trip, how it bonds your heart to those you serve. When you leave, part of you remains behind and a sustained vision of them returns with you.

Brittani shared that the news of their tragedy grieved her deeply: "I lay in bed the whole day and cried!" She confessed. Her husband, Michael, checked on her and asked how he could pray for her. Her response was a grief-stricken one. "My family is hurting". I'm touched when I think of it. Oh, that we would feel our feet again in the body of Christ. Our missionaries are strong and bold, and they feel the pain of "feet." Will we join them from where we are, pleading as Brittani did because "our family is hurting"?

When I taught at Gateway Christian School, I was blessed every morning by my Bible class. During our Morning Prayer time, one young lady named Megan always offered a plea for the babies facing abortion that day. She later extended her requests to include the mothers considering the act of abortion. She prayed that they would have the understanding that they were carrying a precious life inside of them (Psalms 139:13-14). Another student persistently prayed for Israel and Jerusalem. It blessed me to know these students pray continually for the body of Christ, especially those who are persecuted.

We have dear friends who stand in the gap and speak for the persecuted. Doug and Joli Cullen walk by faith day after day and week after week. Their plea is for the churches to hear the cry of the unborn, the elderly, and all those who are too weak to defend their own existence. I am amazed by their dedication to live in an RV and travel extensively for those whom they may never know, yet whose burden they cannot set aside. May God bless those sweet shoes of mercy they wear as they encourage others to choose life. May we too feel the burdens of the persecuted and with heaven's compassion take to them the shoes of mercy.

# Day Five

# Mercy's Shoes

"Then said he also to him that bade him, when thou makest a dinner or supper, call not thy friends, nor thy brethren, neither thy kinsmen, nor thy rich neighbors; lest they also bid thee again, and a recompense be made thee. But when thou makest a feast, call the poor, the maimed, the lame, the blind; and thou shalt be blessed; for they cannot recompense thee: for thou shalt be recompensed at the resurrection of the just."
Luke 14: 12-14

In studying this passage in the gospel of Luke, who were to be the honored guest?

_____

_____

_____

_____

We have learned much this week about mercy's shoes. Today, we conclude by looking through the portals of time and getting a glimpse of the eternal rewards for wearing such shoes. Remember, with every shoe we have put on in this study, there was a shoe to put off. In order to walk in these special shoes of mercy, we must first remove the shoes of personal pursuits.

Observe the following scriptures. What groups of people does God list as priorities in these verses?

_____

_____

Matthew 25: 34-25

34"Then shall the King say unto them on his right hand, come, ye blessed of my Father, inherit the kingdom prepared for you from the foundation of the world: 35for I was an hungered, and ye gave me meat: I was thirsty, and ye gave me drink: I was a stranger, and ye took me in: 36naked and ye clothed me: I was sick and ye visited me: I was in prison, and ye came unto me."

The questions that will be asked at the foot of the throne give insight to the priorities of kingdom work. In one word, the answer is compassion. I must ask myself the question: Do I daily have a Christlike compassion? Are my days driven by my errands or God's? As we observe the ministries of Jesus while on the earth, we see a perfect heart of love.

I remember one Thanksgiving, as a new pastor's wife, I asked God to show me someone who needed help that day. Later, as I was carrying out my stay-at-home, wifely chores, our phone rang. The voice on the other end of the line sounded quite sad. "Ma'am, I was wondering if we could get a little help." As he shared his need, I could sense that this one was sincere. My heart rejoiced with how God had cleared the way for me to know of a desperate little family that could use a lot of love.

On another occasion, I gave a young woman a ride home, after seeing her small frame along the side of the road. She was soaked from a sudden downpour of rain. This time, I was more hesitant about helping than excited. "Can I give you a ride?" I asked. "Yes," responded the frail pedestrian. For all of you mothers and grandmothers reading this, it was a risk I know (even fourteen years ago), but I learned something from that little lady. The lesson stays with me today. She had issues—many of them—and I offered to return the next day with food from our church pantry. I did. I knocked on her door and heard a very weak "Come in." Then I entered to see one of the most pitiful rooms I have ever seen. Turning my sight toward the one I had come to help, I could see her Bible opened in front of her. There she sat quoting a portion of the scripture I had left her with the day before. She agreed to get help, and I drove her to a facility. All the way there, she rocked back and forth quoting that tiny portion of God's Word again and again. I had told her it was her lifeline, and she, with the least amount of strength, was clinging to it. Though she was often in my prayers, I never saw her again. However, the image of her cradling God's Word and constantly repeating His promise stays in my heart. It made me ashamed that I myself have such a wealth of scripture and often fail to cling to it as she.

I must wonder what it would be like to be in their shoes—lonely, afraid, without hope. That's what mercy does, does it not? Mercy takes time to imagine the other's pain, and she walks in their shoes. Mercy stops to invite the unlikely in. That is what we see in our introductory verse for today. You can glance back at it at the first portion of today's study (Luke 14:12-14).

The latter part of those scriptures tells us not to expect them to repay. Instead, God will repay. Can you imagine that—how God repays? Not that we look to be repaid, but what an incredible promise. We read in Luke 14:14, "And thou shalt be blessed: for they cannot recompense thee: for thou shalt be recompensed at the resurrection of the just."

Proverbs 19:17 is an Old Testament connection that also states this promise: "He that hath pity upon the poor lendeth unto the Lord; and that which he hath given will he pay him again."

Chances are you don't get invited to too many celebrations where the guest of honor is the most cast down fellow or gal in the neighborhood. The mindset of the world is far below that of the Lord. We go for the here and now—what looks good and who can make us look good. However, that is not where the joy of life resides. Most of life's joys will be in helping the "least of these" (Mt. 25:40).

George Mueller was an outstanding host to the poor. While ministering to the people of his town, he once said, "This morning, I felt that we should do something for the poor.... I longed to establish a school for the boys and girls, read scriptures to them, and speak to them about the Lord."[1] George Mueller indeed did something for those children. He obeyed God in opening an orphan house and, as our key verse for the day instructed, he "bade" those poor to come to the table. The interesting part of his story was that Bro. Mueller many times invited them to the table without knowing where the meal would come from. In our homes, we set down and bless the food we see before us. George Mueller sat down with his orphan children and blessed the food before it came. To read his daily diary entries is a life-changing experience. He gives account after account of daily prayers asking God to somehow send the milk and food the orphans would need for the next meal. In written detail, Mr. Mueller tells how God specifically met each need. Meal by meal and day by day, this great man of God brought the children to the table and lent to the Lord.

I'm so thankful Jesus invited me to his table. Once spiritually poor and lame, now here I sit daily at the King's banquet. I am blessed and knowing this, I dare not eat my bread alone. My prayer is for my daily bread, both spiritually and physically to be broken and shared with the ones no one wants to invite.

I hope we can gather from this chapter that the poor, the prodigal, the paralyzed, and the persecuted are to be our priority and not our problem. The orphan, widow, imprisoned, lost and outcast must capture our hearts, and they will if we are walking with Jesus in his shoes of mercy.

# WEEK SEVEN

## The Savior's Shoes

# Day One

## As the Lamb of God, He Comes to Be My Sacrifice

"He it is who coming after me is preferred before me, Whose shoe's latchet I am not worthy to unloose." John 1:27

We now come to the most amazing shoes of all times—the Savior's shoes. What a servant's story they could tell if only we could hear them speak. These shoes are the epitome of all we have studied. They are the perfect shoes of grace, the restful shoes of worship, the strongly built shoes of warfare, the wedding shoes of covenant, the walking shoes of ministry, and the serving shoes of mercy all woven together in one. No wonder John felt unworthy to unlatch these shoes.

There are many people in my life that I highly respect and deeply love. My days have been blessed by simply knowing them. Experiences, memories, investments, sacrifices, joys, and tears have bonded our souls. The longer I live, the more I realize what great gifts the Lord has given me in the relationships that surround my life.

I've felt safe under my dad's protection. He's always been my hero. Growing up as a pastor's daughter has been a great joy of learning God's truths. Though now separated by miles, when I call with a question, Dad is still there to teach me about God's Word. I love him dearly, and even the sight of his shoes brings a smile. Then, too, words cannot describe the treasure of my mother. Bible scholar, prayer warrior, sweet humble servant, dedicated wife and mother would be a start. She's the most beautiful servant of God, and I love her. Even seeing her shoes humbles my heart. I can tell, too, of my brothers: they were always there to protect me. They are the ones who share childhood memories, family experiences, and funny stories. We walked together during our formative years and through our teens. I miss them now, but when I'm in for a visit, even a glimpse of those size 12-plus shoes brings treasured memories.

Others who have become a part of my heart and who have deeply influenced me are my husband's family. They are amazingly thoughtful. Whether a brother-in-law or sister-in-law, each time I see them, I see the shoes of service. Emma Lee Howell, my mother-in-law, is such a strong and honest lady. She is eighty-one and she still looks sharp when she steps out, and even the sight of her stylish shoes brightens my thoughts. My father-in-law now waits for us in heaven, but what a worker he was. He had such a dedicated heart, and even seeing his shoes that were passed down to my husband brings a thought of respect. Then there are my three precious girls; I still have their first footprints and baby shoes. They have grown up to far excel our hopes and dreams of Christian young ladies. At times, even seeing their shoes brings me to a time of thanksgiving and praise where I pause and say, "Thank you, Lord, for the special gifts of these sweet girls, for watching over and guiding their steps, and for the promise that you will see them through until they are home."

And how dear are the shoes of my best friend and soul mate. Billy has led me and walked alongside of me for over twenty years. He is the honesty of his mother, the diligent worker of his dad, and the heartfelt preacher of his Lord. I thank God for Billy Howell, my godly husband; even the sight of his polished Sunday shoes stirs my heart to remember how God brings us good and perfect gifts.

The people who hold the highest regards in our heart can but appear before us, and the sight of their presence can bring us to deep emotion. When we have been separated from them for a time, the tenderness ever increases.

Consider John the Baptist when the feet of the Messiah appeared before him. John's confession was that he was not even worthy to unlatch the Messiah's sandals. Upon baptizing Jesus, John saw the confirmation of the Spirit descending like a dove, and he was convinced that Jesus was the Messiah. While in the womb, John's incomplete being had leapt in response to Mary's greeting. Elizabeth rejoiced and the babe within her as well at the mere presence of the Messiah in Mary's womb. By the time of his adult life, John makes an exclamatory statement. With all his being, he now boldly proclaims, "Behold: the Lamb of God!"

Find the text: John 1:35 and write it below.

_____

_____

_____

I'm sure Elizabeth and Zacharias must have ingrained the promise of a coming Messiah into the heart and soul of their Jewish son. Imagine the building anticipation in the mind of John as he learned that God had called him to be the one to prepare the way of the long-awaited Messiah. John had memorized these prophetic promises. They were a part of his formative thoughts. Every obedient Jewish boy memorized the Torah and the scrolls. Now, John's job would be to cry out and to proclaim the coming of the promised Redeemer he had read of so many times. You would think emotion might have overtaken John by the time he actually saw the Messiah with his own eyes. How did he keep from "coming unglued"? How did he stop himself from taking hold of the shoulders of those nearby and shaking them back and forth while looking them in the eye and exclaiming, "Don't you hear?" "Behold the Lamb of God!" "He is here!" Maybe he did. We do see an exclamation point in some areas of the gospel of John. Yet, somehow, I wonder if maybe he was in awe at first. What John experienced went beyond an impulsive, emotional, exclamatory shout. We see a man of God carrying out his faithful mission and proclaiming his consistent message—day after day: "Prepare the way of the Lord. He's coming, and He will take away the sin of the world."

Finally, one day, as John was faithfully sharing God's message, Jesus appears and requests that John baptize Him. John must have been in awe. I imagine it to be one of those times when amazement goes deeper than an exclamation point. I think it more to be an all-encompassing silence and a still type of amazement. Ever been there?

A short time ago, I held a little miracle. Her mother had been told that she had only a two percent chance of ever conceiving again. Fertility means didn't work, and this young mother was devastated. We prayed, asking God to intervene. We asked the Lord to grant a child to this sweet young lady. However, we asked his will be done. As she surrendered the whole situation to God, she began to walk closely with her Lord and was assured that the Lord was her Shepherd.

Months later, my friend sat down beside me just before church service began and said, "Mrs. Howell, guess what?" After naming off a few things we had been praying over, she finally had to help me: "I'm pregnant," she said. I was excited beyond words. Part of me wanted to go run a couple of laps around the sanctuary (I'm sure that would have got the service off to an interesting start), but instead, I just sat ... in awe. Behold, the Lamb of God who has come to do the "impossible."

Months later, my daughter ran through our house calling to me. Pointing to a picture on her cell phone, she said, "Mother, look! Leslie had her baby!" We had been praying for her all day and upon seeing this newborn's picture, I dropped to my knees and whispered with tear-filled eyes, "Thank you, God!" Our answered prayer had a face: ten toes, ten fingers, and beautiful dark hair. She is beautiful! Later that day as I held little Madison Elise Taylor, I stood in amazement.

Behold the Lamb of God who takes away the pain of a barren womb! Have you experienced his glory lately? Prepare. The one you have longed to know all of your Christian life is here. Get ready. He has come to you to take away your troublesome burdens. He will replace them with joy. Any sin can be forgiven. Any sorrow can be redeemed.

If you have been a born-again Christian for any amount of time, you have more than likely experienced this awe. Would you take time now to write about that time in your life? If you feel led, maybe you could also share with your study group? John proclaimed, "Behold the Lamb of God!" As we close today, would you testify with John?

Fill in the following blank in with your own personal reference to the Lamb of God.
(Who is He to you?)

Behold the Lamb of God who _____

_____

Jesus met John down by the Jordan as John was faithfully calling for all to clear the way for the coming of the Messiah. The shoes of the Savior meet us at our area of ministry and lead us to the deeper waters of our faith.

# Day Two

# Shoes of a Shepherd

"The Lord is my Shepherd"
Psalm 23:1

## In the Shoe of the Shepherd, He Comes to My Valley

The most perfect feet wore the most humble shoes. The thought of John unlatching his Messiah's sandal brought John to a most humble state. Why would the sight of shoes bring him to emotion? Simply, shoes reflect the one who wears them, do they not? The shoes of an individual hold the story of their steps; they portray the wearing of their burden. Oh, what the shoes of the Savior could share!

Before his birth, Jesus' perfect feet had walked the portals of glory! Passing through time and space, they left the pathways of perfection and came to walk upon our sinful soil. He cared so much for us that he left heaven. The son of God then walked the path of obedience in his Jewish home. He traveled as all Jewish boys to the synagogue to learn God's Word. Jesus frequented the carpenter's shop to help his dad, and his feet climbed the hill of the city, Jerusalem, to see and take part in sacrifice before the altar.

His shoes held the sand of the desert mountain as He endured temptation and fasted. His sandals traveled the lonely roads to Jericho in order to heal the blind and the cast down. They traveled the Galilean seashore preaching and healing. If we could see supernaturally, we would understand His omnipresence. His shoe prints were at creation along with His father and the Holy Spirit. Jesus has been present at our lowest points and our greatest times of need. His feet walked to the cross and they were nailed there for you and for me. Maybe we have failed to see His faithful footprints in our valley of desperation. Maybe we have let Satan lie to us during our sorrow and tell us that the Savior wasn't there or that he didn't care. For the child of God, the truth is: He was always there. Our Lord was there in our past, He is here in our present, and He will be there in our future.

The enemy will always try to cover up the Savior's footprints. Yet the truth is—Jesus has been there all the while. He cries with us in our pain and longs to comfort us. He desires to work all our sorrows out for good and to trade our defeats for triumphs. One Hebrew name for God is "Jehovah Shammah," which means "He is there." What wonderful promises are wrapped in His name. It brings me comfort to know He is there, and that He will never leave. If you have trouble seeing God in the pages of your life, go back as I have and ask Him to reveal His footprints in your valley. The Savior's shoes were there. They were underneath your willow tree of mourning. I can testify to it. Good News: They are still there waiting to walk you to joy. Come see, "Behold the Lamb of God, who takes away the sin of the world." He will take away your pain. They are there, too, in your future, already there to lead you and guide you. He is there seeing the completed work of your life and telling you to relax and remember that your life is His work and He will complete it as you surrender to Him (Phil 1:6). Have you ever seen times when young children caught a ride on their dad's feet? Placing each foot on top of Dad's shoes, their feet moved under his power. All they had to do was place their feet on his and be ushered up and away as He made the strides for them. Loving hearts live to guide others. Perhaps the best ways to illustrate this fact of God's abiding presence is by way of the illustration of a shepherd.

One loving title chosen by our Savior was that of the "Good Shepherd." He chose this title as a personal reference to his relationship with us. As we consider the shoes of our Savior, we can't miss those humble shepherd's shoes. First of all, the "Lamb of God" left the safety of Heaven to guide you and me to green pastures and still waters. He put on the shoes of a shepherd and came to us. Secondly, we can find his footprints in our wilderness valleys. We see them beside the den of the lion as he came to rescue us from the mouth of the enemy. Finally, tracing this trail of the shepherd's shoe prints, we are assured he is already there in our future with goodness and mercy.

As we take a look today at Psalms 23, we see some deeply embedded shoe prints near a gentle flowing stream. They are no doubt those left by the shepherd and his water-soaked sandals. Taking the time to wade through the waters and encourage the sheep's trust is a wet job at times. As we know, sheep don't like fast-running water.

233

They are skittish animals and very fearful. Knowing the frightful state of his sheep, one of the shepherd's priorities is to quite the fretful ones by leading them by "still waters" (Ps. 23:2). However, when it is necessary for the sheep to cross over the waters, the shepherd remains close by, ever watching them over to the other side. Many times in my life, I have feared the waters. Waters of worry rush over this mother's heart. Waves of anxiety seem to loom at every side. "How will my girls stand in such an evil day?" "What if something should happen to my mate?" "What if people keep falling away from church?" How sweet it is to hear the voice of my shepherd say, "When thou passest through the waters, I will be with thee; and through the rivers, they shall not overflow thee: when thou walkest through the fire, thou shalt not be burned; neither shall the flame kindle upon thee" (Isaiah 43:2). Yes, the shoe prints of my shepherd are there, beside the waters.

Then, too, it makes all the difference to have a shepherd in your valley. Going into a dark and threatening environment is bad enough, but to go there vulnerable could be death. The beloved twenty-third chapter of Psalms is more than a reading of comfort at funerals and graveside services. These promises written by the shepherd, David, are encouraging insights from an experienced heart of a shepherd.

Record some of the comforts the psalmist describes in Psalm 23.

_____

_____

_____

_____

Now, fill in the missing words from Psalm 23:4

"Yea, though I walk _____ the valley of the shadow of death, I will fear no evil: for _____ art _____ me; thy rod and thy staff they comfort me."

We often question our shepherd why we must walk <u>through</u> the valley. However, we all must go to our valley and walk through. Not by, not around, but through our valley we must go. Thankfully, however, we never walk our valley alone. Our Shepherd walks on ahead, and he guards from behind as well. The valleys are deep, aren't they? It takes a long while to walk *through* them. Sometimes, it may even seem that our Shepherd is not there, but he is. Closer than we know he is there, quietly planning our paths to tomorrow's green pastures. He is there, all through the night, guarding and watching. He is the Good Shepherd, and he loves His sheep.

I have questioned my valleys, have you? Not disrespectfully, but earnestly, I asked my Shepherd, "Why the valley?" "Where were you in that awful dark time?" I asked my Lord. "I thought I would perish there," I continued. In a most tender way, he answered me, "We must go back to the valley for this answer, my dear one." I cried in response, "Please, not back to the valley!" However, this time, we returned to the valley in the light of day. As I stood at the place of my fear, my shepherd pointed to something in the ground. He gently led me to the prints of His dear Shepherd's shoes that still remained in my valley to this day. They were there! The place that held one of my greatest fears also held His footprints. "I never knew those were there," I said to my Shepherd. "I was always there," he assured. "I was here crying with you as you had to endure this horrible time. Now it is time for you to evermore see this valley as it really is, my redeemed one," he said. "With My Word I set you free," He proclaimed. The words from II Timothy 1:7 swept through my mind with an almighty redeeming power of truth: "For God hath not given us the spirit of fear; but of power, and of love, and of a sound mind." "Look around my lamb, this is your valley, it holds nothing but peace now. The willows here softly sing of your sorrow, and the lilies loudly trumpet your victory. No more will you fear this valley, but here you will forever more proclaim freedom from your darkness. I am your Shepherd, and I stand with all authority in your valley." You will now walk here among lilies; your valley will forever more bloom. I have claim to this ground, and I am your Shepherd.

Lovingly, the shoes of the Shepherd come to our valleys to extend beauty for ashes and hope for despair.

# Day Three

## From Shoes of the Carpenter
## to Shoes of the Fisherman
## As Carpenter, He Comes to My Home
## As Fisherman, He Meets Me At My Work

Matthew 13:55
"Is not this the Carpenter's son?"

### Shoes of the Carpenter

Have you ever wondered why the Savior came in the shoes of a carpenter? The shoes of the Carpenter came to meet us at our homes. He still comes today with the perfect blueprint for each life. No matter the condition, the Carpenter sent from above can rebuild any home. He provided the materials at His own expense, and every board is nailed with love.

Jesus, our Savior, comes in carpenter's shoes. He comes to build lives and homes. Taking on the task of building lives, the Carpenter from glory has the perfect blueprints. First of all, He has the foundation. Secondly, He knows all about repair. Finally, He has the perfect material.

I remember well the first time I saw the Carpenter's feet at my home. With me a young girl, he came dressed a lot like our first pastor,

Bro. George Carneal. He invited us to come to church as a family. His wife sat down with me on their front porch steps and showed me the blueprints. They were written by a man named Paul who wrote them in a letter entitled "Romans." That Sunday evening, I decided to turn my life over to the Carpenter. Since that day, He has been here in my home. He is a faithful carpenter. When I am not even aware, He is working. He never leaves. As a matter of fact, He has promised to finish the work He started, and I know He will. I have seen Him build other lives. Men and women that once seemed broken and in shambles are now masterpieces of this Master Carpenter.

After setting my foundation as a child, God continued to build walls of communication and identity in my teens through good Christian leaders in our churches, Sunday school teachers, and mentors. Later in my life, the grand builder saw that it was time for my covering. That's when he sent my dear husband. Next, it was time to finish the attic and provide a place for memories. Wouldn't you know the master builder knew just what we needed? His carpenter's shoes were there to carve out each beautiful gift complete with curls, smiles, and laughter.

Not only did God build our home, He has carved every life and sweet memory. For example, there is our kitchen table. He contemplated each chair and who would occupy them. He shaped each chair to hold fellowship and laughter. The table He made strong and sturdy to uphold testimonies and advice that would be passed across it from friends and loved ones.

The design He creates and the detail He gives a life is matchless. He finishes the work He begins. "For I know the thoughts that I think toward you, saith the Lord, thoughts of peace, and not of evil, to give you an expected end." Jeremiah 29:11

I must tell you, too, of the Carpenter's compassion. He is patient and kind with His work. I remember one special day when I was feeling quite unfinished——okay, maybe it was more like demolished. As a young wife, I had a day when discouragement filled my mind. I knew I had failed in a number of areas, and guilt feelings tried to block any truth of forgiveness. Walking outside our small apartment, I sat down on the steps in hopes the Lord would clear my heart of the condemning feelings of my soul. Lord, I know I have failed, and I ask forgiveness. Please convince my heart that it is done. As time passed, all was quite. Then, softly, a distant sound suddenly moved from the background of my listening ear to the foreground of my mind. It was the sound of a hammer ringing out. A neighbor was hard at work hammering on some project, and the Carpenter of Heaven was at work nailing down a fact in my heart. I began to smile as I realized what was taking place. The Lord had heard my prayer and in the stillness, I had my answer. With each strike of the hammer, I heard … Forgiven! Nothing can separate you from me … (Romans 8:35, 39). Forgiven! You are mine forever … Forgiven! I have paid the price to complete you. The shoes of the Carpenter appeared at the door of my heart that day and nailed down some truths about forgiveness. I am thankful the shoes of the Savior included the Carpenter's shoes.

Take a moment to read Romans 8:1. Make it a goal this week to commit this verse to memory. Write it out on a note card and place it in a special place.

## Shoes of the Fisherman

Dressed in the shoes of a fisherman, Jesus comes to help with our work. Isn't it a wonder that the Savior, ruler of the world, would come and cover His feet in simple fishermen's sandals to meet us at our place of work? The shoes of the Savior come to our workplace to bring us the same message he brought His followers: "Come, follow me" (Mark 1:17). "Let your work be about My work," He calls. Join me in fishing for men. No matter what your employment is, the call is still the same. Come, let my work be your work.

In looking at the shoes of the Savior that frequented the Galilean shores, we see the perfect instructor for all fields of labor. Jesus met His disciples time after time at their place of work. He first came by the seashore to call them to His kingdom work. As women, we get caught up in our work, don't we? Like Martha, our mound of expectations can get us in a tizzy. Men are often driven by their work as well, while both men and women are driven to find their identity in their work. The great fisherman comes to teach us something different.

Our identity is to be solely in Christ. Work is not to be an avenue to our identity, but an avenue from our identity in Christ. We are complete in Him. Our workplace is to serve as a platform of ministry to others, not a pathway to self-worth for self. If we are not careful, our work can be solely driven by our flesh and not led by God's Spirit. Jesus could have resided in the synagogue and dealt with only the folks who might come to Him there. However, the Great Fisherman chose to come our way and meet us in the daily grind. He chose to come down by our "seashore." He makes a definite decision to encourage us after we have worked all night and caught nothing. Helpfully, He calls out to throw our net to the other side. (It sounds like something we have already tried, but "here goes nothing," we think.) The "nothing" turns out to be a big "something" when we take time to listen to Jesus' plans at our place of work! Jesus knows how to reach us at our work and help to solve our problems, beginning with the reason we work. Our work is to be about His work; it should be always and only for the Kingdom of our God (Matthew 6:33).

Read the following scripture passage. I Peter 5:10.

How does this verse bring comfort to you? _____

_____

_____

_____

Secondly, the Fisherman's shoes come to our workplace to calm our storms. When the storms rage and all seems lost, we can look aside to see the Fisherman's shoes there walking on our waves. Some of our greatest stressors come from our occupations, don't they? Jesus knew we would have a special need for companionship and support in our work, so He planned before the foundations of the world to strap on these sandals of service and help us out of many a difficult work day. He is there by our seaside with nourishment to build us up for the task. Think of it the next time you are exhausted and depleted and still covered up by your work. Hear His words, "Children, Have ye any meat?" (John 21:5) He gently calls to us in our frail state, "Come unto me, all ye that labour and are heavy laden, and I will give you rest" (Matthew 11:28).

Knowing that Jesus cares so much as to help us carry our burden, we should put on His shoes of service and help those around us who are overburdened. The Fisherman has given us the example by the shores of Galilee. Bearing one another's burdens is part of the kingdom call. Come, let us put on the shoes of the Fisherman and follow Him.

# Day Four

## The Great Physician's Shoes: As Physician, He Took My Pain; He Wore the Mourner's Shoes

J esus came to die. From heaven's portal, the Great Physician, came barefoot in uncomfortable human flesh, and he departed in pain, unshod. Our Savior put on the shoes of a shepherd, and he bore the marks of the lowest criminal. Sawdust covered his feet as a carpenter, and he was shod with the common shoes of a fisherman. He entered and exited this world as a mourner—without shoes.

The Old Testament asks the question: "Is there no balm in Gilead; is there no physician there? Why then is not the health of the daughter of my people recovered?" (Jeremiah 8:22)

The New Testament resounds with the answer: "The blind receive their sight, and the lame walk, the lepers are cleansed, and the deaf hear, the dead are raised, and the poor have the gospel preached to them" (Matthew 11:5).

His name is Jesus. He has come, and he wears physician's shoes. Our balm of Gilead, our Great Physician is here! What is so amazing about the Physician's shoe, you ask. Listen closely: The people He helped were supposed to be "helpless," castaways, outcast, unclean. There were many reasons this Great Physician could have stayed away from the ones who approached Him. As a Jewish man and Rabbi, many of these ailments, such as leprosy, issues of blood, and dead bodies were forbidden. Even the lame, blind, and dumb were thought to be untouchable, unclean, and therefore avoided. This would have kept the shoes of the Physician far from touching distance of those in need. However, praise be to God, our Great Physician has more compassion than any earthly story of kindness ever could tell. Remember those times when your mother or grandmother sat by you when you were ill, no matter the threat to their own health. Then, too, there were the long sleepless nights watching over you to make sure you were okay. Love crosses over the barriers. Jesus did. He came near, He looked in the pale eyes, and He touched the fevered brow. He let His whole pure person reach out to the leper's unclean limbs, and He raised the dead back to life.

Jesus knew the other side of suffering. As the physician of all time, he had the remedy for body and soul. At times, He did use practices such as mixing his perfect saliva with the earthly soil to bring blind eyes to see; however, always it was His Word that healed. He called on man to have faith and trust that he could heal their suffering. M.R. Dehaan in his book *Broken Things* addresses the ministry of suffering. He points out that suffering has a great purpose. As he puts it, suffering: "silences the enemy, enables us to glorify God, makes us more like Christ, helps us to be thankful, teaches us to be dependent on God, provides patience and humility, teaches us to pray, and, finally, suffering brings reward." Maybe that is why we will enter Heaven through gates of pearl—sorrow turned precious; there is treasure in suffering as pointed out by Dehaan.[1] Purity to the silver comes by fire, and surely God's purpose is to bring us forth as pure treasures. Any needful suffering is carried out by the most skilled hands and surgery done by the most capable mind.

In the day we live in, we would no doubt rather avoid pain and sorrow. Sickness and suffering have never been the things man longs for; quite the opposite. We are driven to find comfort and peace. For this very reason, some people avoid God. They think that following Him will bring pain and discomfort. True, there is a cost in disciples, but all temporary pain and suffering will be redeemed with eternal spiritual treasures.

Warren Wiersbe helps us to see suffering in a better light. In *Live Like A King,* he writes, "Jesus never tried to escape the sorrows of life. Nor did He deny they existed. He transformed them." He goes on to say, "Natural sorrow expressed in mourning releases a healing process," whereas "people who, for one reason or another, do not mourn, do not easily adjust to new circumstances; their wound never seems to heal."[2]

Perhaps the most difficult pain and grief our Physician helps us with is the loss of a life. It throws us into a plethora of difficult emotions whether we accept them or not. Though sometimes viewed as weakness, mourning is one of the most needful processes we walk through in our life. For our Great Physician and Wonderful Counselor to put aside His shoes of joy and take on the shoes of suffering is a beautiful wonder indeed. I have to wonder: How much do my shoes resemble that of my

Lord? Do others see the shoes of the Savior in my life? If they did, they would see shoes of grace.

When a Jewish man goes through mourning, he intentionally puts off comfort for a designated time. He either goes without shoes (barefoot), wears cloth wrappings over his feet, or at least puts a stone in his shoe so that he is constantly aware of the discipline of mourning.[3] Self-induced discomfort serves as a reminder for one to grieve in the Jewish world.. It presses the human mind to give thought to those who are hurting as well as helping to consider the life that has been lived. Personal denial helps open our mind to thought and reverence of another. A mourner's heart was to hold precious and honor the life that had been lived.

The scriptures describe Jesus as a man of sorrows (Isaiah 53:3). Surely he was, for his heart was often heavy with many forms of loss. Being the source of all joy, it hurt him to see that joy rejected. It was only a grief that He, as our Savior, could know and understand. As a mourner in the Jewish culture positioned himself under the mode of death, the Jewish man as well made himself walk through part of the shadow of death. Jesus met this shadow of death and conquered all the powers it possessed. From the time he was born, he prepared for death. He not only mourned with us over loss, but he also became our loss. Our all-mighty God became sin for us and died in our place. He didn't just mourn with us, he conquered our source of sorrow. What a Savior we have who purposely put on the shoes of mourning to give us joy unspeakable. Our Lord placed on the shoes of the mourner so that we might constantly rejoice! Behold the Lamb of God who takes away our sorrow. Thank you Jesus for walking in the mourner's shoes!

# Day Five

## Shoes Fit for the King;
## As King He Comes To Be My Ransom

Jesus always put aside the self to show mercy and grace. I will never get over the cross. The grace displayed there is more than I can take in. Jesus put aside any tendency to yield to the flesh and strike back when he was stricken. He had mercy. He forgave immediately, even when spat upon and mocked, and He extended grace. He even prayed, "Father forgive them" as they were causing him pain and disgrace (Luke 23:34). Oh, what Mercy! Oh, what Grace! He was Rabbi, Prophet, Priest, and King, yet he stepped down from his places of authorities to become our guilt.

During his own pain, he reached out to help comfort one beside him. —Grace!

While paying for the sin, he forgave the sinners. —Mercy and Grace!

While dying of thirst, he gave men the living water. —Grace!

While hanging in darkness, he gave forth the brightest light. —Mercy!

While rejected from the Father, he accepted you and me. —Grace

While suffering loneliness, He made sure those near him would be cared for. —Mercy

While his feet were sacrificed, my feet were healed. —Grace

The shoes of the Savior are also those of the perfect Rabbi, Prophet, Priest, and King. What an amazing thought to consider our King of Kings, Priest, Perfect Prophet, and Rabbi chose to step down from His place of authority and step into our shoes of flesh.

He came so humbly, the world missed His entrance. Coming unexpectedly by way of a lowly couple in Nazareth, the King of all Kings entered our world. Born not as royalty but in a smelly stable in Bethlehem, the precious person of His majesty allowed his glory to be hidden in order to provide the lowest peasant shoes for the kingdom.

Imagine Jesus as a growing young man, witnessing the local courts of Jewish law. Consider the compassion He felt in his teens. The growing desire to stand and defend the innocent had to be a heavy burden. It was what He was born for. In His heart as He saw the terrible injustice all around him, I am sure a building passion grew in the heart of this King. Surely, a pressing call to rise up and provide justice followed His heart, yet he patiently waited on the Father's timing. He waited on the right time and the right place to fulfill the most profound act of justice of all times. The right time was the darkest time in history, after 400 hundred years of silence. Many lived an empty religion. The world was filled with crime and pride. The backdrop was set for the great God of Heaven to require sin's debt to be paid.

When the time did come, it was the most unusual but, at the same time, the most beautiful court case ever to be witnessed by all Heaven and Earth. High above man's ways, God had planned the perfect courtroom of divine judgment. It was to be on a hill called Calvary, also known as the "place of the skull." There remains a hillside to this day in Jerusalem that plainly resembles a skull. Now imagine this entire scene as I list for you the scenes and sounds of this great outdoor session of court.

**The place of the court:**

A hill naturally carved—resembling a skull

A place known as Jerusalem—the center of human existence—the crossroad of world

A place where God had written His name

A place where God's holy pattern of a temple was built

A place where year after year believer's would come to sacrifice lambs in hopes of a Messiah who would one day come to save them

**The sounds of the court:**

Cursings

Voices screaming, mocking, condemning

Nails

Cries of Pain and thirst

A most humble innocent man calling out for the forgiveness of His
offenders

The sound of a son arranging for His mother's provision in His dying
hours

A mother weeping for her firstborn son

Friends weeping for the most humble, innocent person they had ever
known

A great rumbling as the earth quaked and the rocks cried out

Onlookers screaming due to darkness....finally,

A loud cry proclaiming............ "It is Finished!"

## He Took My Whipping for Me

There was a certain school, among the mountains of Virginia,
which no teacher could  handle. The boys were so rough that
the teachers resigned.

A young, gray-eyed teacher applied, and the old director
scanned him, then said,

"Young fellow, do you know what you are asking? An awful
beatin'! Every teacher we have had for years has had to take
it."

He replied, "I'll risk it."

Finally, he appeared for duty. One big fellow, Tom, whispered,
"I won't need any help,

I can lick him myself!"

The teacher said, "Good morning boys! We have come to conduct school, but I confess

I do not know how unless you help me. Suppose we have a few rules. You tell me and

I will write them on the blackboard."

One fellow yelled, "No stealing." Another yelled, "On time." Finally ten rules appeared.

"Now," said the teacher, "a law is no good unless there is a penalty attached to it. What shall we do with the one who breaks the rules?"

"Beat him across the back ten times without his coat on."

"That is pretty severe, boys. Are you ready to stand by it?" Another yell, and the teacher said, "School come to order!"

In a day or so, "Big Tom" found his dinner was stolen. Upon inquiry the thief was located - a hungry little fellow, about ten years old. The next morning the teacher announced, "We have found the thief and he must be punished according to your rule – ten stripes across the back! Jim, come up here!"

The little fellow, trembling, came up slowly with a big coat fastened up to the neck and pleaded, "Teacher, you can lick me as hard as you like, but please don't make me take my coat off."

"Take that coat off; you helped make the rules."

"Oh, teacher, don't make me!" He began to unbutton, and what did the teacher behold!

Lo, the lad had no shirt on over his little bony body.

"How can I whip this child," thought he. "But I must do something if I keep this school." Everything was quiet as death.

"How do you come to be without a shirt, Jim?"

He replied, "My father died and mother is very poor. I have only one shirt to my name, and she is washing that today, and I wore my brother's big coat to keep warm."

The teacher with rod in hand hesitated. Just then "Big Tom" jumped to his feet and said, "Teacher, if you don't object, I will take Jim's licking for him."

"Very well, there is a certain law that one can become a substitute for another. Are you all agreed?"

Off came Tom's coat, and after five hard strokes the rod broke! The teacher bowed his head in his hands, and thought, "How can I finish this awful task?"

Then he heard the entire school sobbing, and what did he see? Little Jim had reached up and caught Tom with both arms around his neck. "Tom, I am sorry I stole your dinner, but I was awful hungry. Tom, I'll love you till I die for taking my licking for me! Yes, I'll love you forever!"[4]

- quote from *Echoes of Grace – How Great is His Beauty*

"He was wounded for our transgressions, He was bruised for our iniquities: the chastisement of our peace was upon Him; and with His stripes we are healed. All we like sheep have gone astray; we have turned every one to his own way; and the Lord hath laid on Him the iniquity of us all." Isa.53:5, 6.

John knew that when the Messiah made himself known, he, John, would not even feel worthy enough to approach him as a servant or a slave. John's continuous confession was, "I am not, but He is." John had the right respect for the Lord. He saw his majesty. He knew what the term "Messiah" would entail. John saw through the simple leather sandals to the coverings of the King of all kings and Lord of all lords. His majesty was about to be before him, and John rightfully felt unworthy.

Mary and Martha knew Him as Lord as well. As I've heard it said in a sermon by Dr. William Boyd Bingham of the Binghamtown Baptist Church, "Mary had the right position, and Martha had the right profession". In Luke 10:39, Mary was at His feet. Then too, Martha had the correct profession, "thou art the Christ" (John 11:27). Once we really see Jesus for who he is, we will bow and gladly humble our hearts before His wonderful presence. If we but could see the scars, we would as Thomas express, "My Lord and my God." Heavens courts have no foolish reservations to His praise. They worship in resounding glory and praise to the Lamb of God who takes away the sin of the world. Babies in the womb reflect his glory. They declare Him as

Creator before they utter a word—just by their wonderful and marvelous design and wonder. Trees clap their hands, and rocks stand ready to cry out. They have the sounds and miracles of all time recorded in their substance. Oh what they could shout. All of creation longs to be restored and sing His praises without flaw. He is Majesty, and our place is at His feet.

Our precious Savior is every joy we will ever pursue. He is every covering we long to have. He is our shoes of grace, our worship, our standing in warfare, our covenant, our walk, our mercy, and our joy. May we each day put on Christ and walk with Him in His shoes of Grace, the Savior's shoes.

"Behold the Lamb of God, who takes the sins of the world." Even the sight of His shoes brings me to bow.

# Appendix

## Week 1
## Shoes of Grace

## Background Scripture: Genesis 3 and 4
## Key Passage: Genesis 3:6-7; 21

Background information for "Shoes of Grace"

Each week, we will focus on accepting the shoes God offers us in exchange for the burdensome shoes we walk in. Walking with God requires spiritual shoes. Thankfully, the lessons we learn from Biblical shoes teach us how to walk in harmony with our Savior. This week, we see Eve step into the high heels of low living (Gen. 3:6-7). The cost and loss was great for this terrible step aside from God. Finally, she must put these shoes of the flesh off and put on the shoes of grace in order to once again walk with a most Holy God. When man and woman had committed the sins that would lead to all sins, God lovingly provided a covering of grace (Gen. 3:21).

Creative ways to present Week One in a group study:

- Make a sign, "Shoes of Grace for Shoes of Guilt," with red lettering. (Red representing our redemptive covering provided through the cross.)

- Display a pair of red shoes/ slippers to emphasize the "Ruby Red Shoes of Grace" we are offered through Jesus.

- Display a pair of black shoes to represent the shoes of the flesh that every person should set aside in exchange for grace.

- Make bookmarks shaped like shoes. Add your key scripture passage on the back. Laminate, trim, and use a hole punch to make a hole for yarn or ribbon trim.

- Provide an inexpensive pocket folder for each person with paper for notes. Add label on the front of the folders with clip art of shoes.

Key Questions to discuss in group time:
1. What lies did Satan use to present the shoes of the flesh?
2. What proof does the Bible give in Genesis that sin results in a separated walk with God? (Where were they when God came to walk with them?)

# Week 2
## Shoes of Worship

## Background Reading: Exodus 3
## Key Passage: Exodus 3:5

Background information for "Shoes of Worship":

The shoes we exchange this week are "Shoes of Worry for Shoes of Worship" (Regret for Rest). Moses regretted the fact that he had been unable to set his people free while he was a ruler in Egypt. However, surrendering his shoes of worry in exchange for worship provided him with the right covering he would need to return. This time, he would deliver in God's strength, and the captives would come out with a mighty hand. We follow Moses to the mountain to see him step aside to see God, step out of what he stood on to worship God, and step into God's Shoes of worship to deliver his hurting people. Worship enables us to rest and rely on God's strength to carry out His work.

Creative Ways to Present Week Two in a Group Study:

- Make a sign that reads "Shoes of Worship for Shoes of Worry" written in blue. (Blue representing the rest that comes through worship.)

- Extend a notice/ invitation/ announcement informing the attendees to come in to the study wearing their house shoes. This will help emphasize the theme of "Shoes of Rest and Worship."

- Make a few "Worship Baskets" to give away as door prizes. Items could include: house shoes, comfy socks, notes of encouragement written by ladies of the Bible study group, Christian music CDS, devotional books, etc...)

Key Questions to discuss in group time.
1. What was Moses doing when he saw the bush aflame?
2. What did God's call to Moses require?
3. What regret had Moses lived with for forty years?

After a time of questions and discussion, ask for those ladies present to share times when God took them from the pits to praise. Be prepared, as the facilitator, to share some special times of worship that you have experienced.

\* For every fleshly shoe that we "put off," God will give us Spiritual shoes to "put on." These shoes will be the coverings we need to do the spiritual task God has called us to do.

# Week 3

## Shoes of Warfare

## Background Scripture: Joshua 5:13-15; 6:1-16
## Key Passages: Joshua 5:13-15

Background information for "Shoes of Warfare":

Joshua was a mighty warrior, yet he could not fight the walled city of Jericho in his own strength. This mighty warrior was approached by the angel of the Lord's host and told to remove his shoes. Joshua had to put aside his shoes of self-reliance and put on God's shoes of warfare in order to take the stronghold of Jericho. Joshua had to surrender his plans and seek God's orders. As in Proverbs 3:5-6, the requirement is to trust God and not lean on one's own thoughts or plans. This is the only way to have true victory.

Creative ways to present Week Three in a group session:

- Decorate with camouflage or army green colors. Write out "Shoes of Peace for Shoes of Presumption" in green.

- Encourage those attending to wear boots. Camouflage or army clothing might also be worn.

- Spray paint an old pair of shoes with camouflage colors and patterns.

- Have an outline of a shoe available for each person. Ask them to draw a picture of their "foe" (emotion or stronghold they are fighting) on the bottom of their paper-made "Shoe of Warfare." Example: "fear of tomorrow" or "worry over finances" may be written or drawn on the bottom of their shoe.

- Fold all of the written fears and strongholds and place them in the center of the room. Gather in a circle around the piled stronghold and pray over your Jericho stones.

- Provide small squares of paper for each person. Have everyone write their name on their slips of paper and pass it to the person on their right. Ask each one to pray over their name for the next week.

Questions to Consider for "Shoes of Warfare":

1. Can you describe the military plan God gave Joshua?
2. Why would this be a hard plan to follow?
3. Has God ever asked you to do something that seemed difficult to do?

# Week 4

# Wedding Shoes

## Background Scripture: Ruth 1-4
## Key Passages: Ruth 4:7-8

Background information for "Wedding Shoes":

Naomi and her husband, Elimelech, left Bethlehem due to a famine in their land. They went down to a pagan city, Moab, for food, and only planned to stay there to sojourn (visit). However, the family settled there, and each son took a Moabite woman as his wife. Sadly, Naomi's husband and sons died in Moab, leaving Naomi without anyone to protect her or provide for her needs. She decides to go back home, and is accompanied by one of her daughter-in-laws, Ruth. Vulnerable, lonely, and insecure, Naomi and Ruth travel back to Bethlehem. In Bethlehem, Ruth is taken to be the wife of Boaz. This comes after a nearer kinsman decides he will not take in Ruth. The custom of that day was to take off your shoe and give it to another if you surrendered your rights of land or a brother's widow. The next of kin could then accept the shoe and claim the position of provider and protector.

Creative ways to present Week Four to a study group:

- Create a sign that reads "Shoes of Covenant for Shoes of Insecurity" in a silver colored marker, paint, or print.

- Display white wedding shoes or white dress shoes.

- Have ladies to bring photographs of their wedding. Ask a few volunteers to share unique promises they remember from their vows.

- If your group collects an outreach offering, consider using this to give a money gift or gift card toward wedding shoes for a bride-to-be. A copy of "Shoes in the Bible and Walking with God" could be added along with this as a Bible study outreach. (You may want to place a book mark in chapter 4, "Wedding Shoes.")

Key Questions to Discuss during group time:

1. What emotions did Naomi experience as she returned to Bethlehem?

2. As widows, how were Ruth and Naomi vulnerable and needy?

3. What was the significance of the shoe that Boaz used to claim Ruth?

# Week 5

# Walking Shoes

## Background Scriptures: Mark 6:8-11; II Corinthians 5:7; Galatians 5:25; Ephesians 4:1; and Ephesians 5:15

## Key Passages: II Corinthians 5:7 and Mark 6:8

Background information on "Walking Shoes":

As we live or "walk" in this world, we are called to do so in a spiritual manner (Gal. 5:25). Our vocation should show forth a walk of faith (Ephesians 4:1-3). Our manner of response to life circumstances should show forth patience. We are to walk "circumspectly" (Eph. 5:15). "Circumspectly" means separated from the worldly walk. The worldly system entices us to walk by sight. Sight-walking demands for black and white, concrete facts to lead us—working to provide our need, manipulating circumstances and people to get what we want, living to get temporary things, mapping out our own plans and depending on self to "make it happen, now." Faith-walking calls for praying—asking God's plans for our day, believing he can do amazing things, seeking his provisions for the impossible, and waiting on God to instruct us on how to complete the work. It is focused on giving and not getting. It is willing to wash feet and shake off rejection. When we obey God and walk by faith, we will exchange "Shoes of Sight for Shoes of Faith."

Ideas for presenting "Walking Shoes" creatively in a group study:

- Create a sign with "Shoes of Faith for Shoes of Sight" written in gold. Gold helps us to remember that we live for a heavenly eternal kingdom and not toward temporary earthly riches that soon pass away.

- If you wanted to contrast the two shoes, you could set out dark brown shoes to represent the earthly shoes of sight and glittery gold shoes could be used to illustrate the Christian's shoes of faith.

- Gift certificates for walking shoes (tennis shoes) could be given as door prizes. Random sizes of cute tennis shoes could be purchased with bowls in front of each size for those who would like to sign up for a drawing in their size category. Note: Shoes with scripture verses can be ordered as special gift ideas. Computer searches should easily assist you in accessing these shoes. (I searched "shoes with scripture" and found several choices.)

Discussion questions from Chapter 4:

1. When was the last time you stepped out in faith to do something only God could do?

2. How can we "wash feet" spiritually?

3. What does it mean to "shake the dust" off your spiritual shoes?

Week 6

Shoes of Mercy

Background Scripture: Luke 14:12-14;
Luke 10:29-37; Acts 3:1-8
Key Passages: Luke 10: 36-37 and Luke 14:13

Background information on "Shoe of Mercy":

Just as in our day, there were many poor in Biblical times. The poor and needy have a special place in the heart of God. Though sometimes it is difficult to identify a real need from an idle beggar, God gives us defining list of those we need to assist, such as: the widow without family, the fatherless, and the poor who cannot work due to sincere disabilities. His Word also defines those who we should not enable to idleness whom the Bible identifies as sluggards (lazy people). The capable who can work should work (II Thessalonians 3:10). In addition, His Holy Spirit moves on our heart to guide us in individual circumstances. God wants us to show mercy and not to be a respecter of persons. Mercy can be given by way of a visit to those in prison, visiting the sick, or simply giving to help a financial need.

Creative ways to teach "Shoes of Mercy" in a group study:

- Display sign with "Shoes of Mercy for Shoes of Misery" in orange.

- Identify local needs in reference to the Biblical list that was identified this week in your study. Consider collecting needs or giving a money gift to a local Children's Home.

- Teach this study in a prison ministry as a way of offering shoes of mercy to the shoeless.

- Plan a trip to a local shoe store with a needy child and purchase them shoes.

- Teach this study to your family at home as a way of walking together in the shoes of mercy, beginning with family fellowship.

- Purchase tracts to give out to the lost you come in contact with. Make sure to have gospel tracts with you when you are out to eat or traveling. I keep them in my purse and the glove compartment of our van. Be sure to keep copies of church bulletins as well.

- Ask folks you come in contact with how you can pray for them.

Group discussion questions for "Shoes of Mercy":

1. Who are the paralyzed?
2. Who are the persecuted?

3.  Consider the hurting on the Jericho road, the prodigals in the hog pen, and the widow in her lonely home. How can you reach them?

## Week 7

## The Shoes of the Savior

### Background Scriptures: John13:1-17; I Peter 2:21-25
### Key Scripture for Group Discussion: I Peter 2:21

Background information: Jesus stepped away from His heavenly home. He came down and put on earthly shoes so that we could step into His shoes of grace, worship, victory, covenant, fellowship, compassion, and love. He paid the cost of our walk with God:

As the Lamb of God, He is our sacrifice;

As Shepherd, He comes to our valley;

As Carpenter, He comes to our home; as fisherman to our place of work;

As Physician he is there at our sick bed, and

As the one just King of kings, He became our injustice, and He is our righteousness.

Creative ways to present "The Shoes of the Savior":

*   Make a sign with the phrase "Shoes of Comfort for Shoes of Suffering" in pink.

- Ask God to give you twelve ladies to mentor throughout the next year.

- Take time to help a younger Christian in her occupation, church roles, and personal growth. You may want to meet her for lunch breaks, offer child care, or send an encouraging note.

- Invite a new family over for dinner.

- Make "Shoes in the Bible" baskets to give away as a form of outreach and encouragement. Women need the Word of God, and God has given us the gift of creativity to wrap up His Word and deliver it to a hungry world.

**Possible items for Bible study baskets include**:

*Shoes in the Bible and Walking With God* Bible study book

A creative bookmark (a shoe cutout, flip-flops) to represent each week of study.

Music CD

Church Bulletin and Gospel Tract

Group questions for "Shoes of the Savior":

1. How does our church practice walking in the Shepherd's shoes?
2. What are some creative ways we can support others in their work?

3. How are we reaching out to the sick and the imprisoned? Are we willing to cross some boundaries of comfort to reach out to their need?

# RESOURCES

## Week 1

[1]Purdom, Dr. Georgia "The Amazing Regenerating Rib" *Answers in Genesis.* http://www.answersingenesis.org/articles/aid/v4'nl/regenerating rib (accessed December 30 2012).

## Week 2

[1]Easton, M.C. "Backside of the Desert" *BibleStudyTools.com.* biblestudytools.com/dictionary/desert (accessed December 30 2012).

[2]Brabson, Fredrick E. Sermon from series *"The Urgency of Doubles.* Knoxville, Tn.37950-0588: Relevant Ministries, A Ministry of New Covenant Baptist Church.

[3]Parsons, John J. "Hebrew Names of God" *Hebrew for Christians.* http//www.hebrew4christians.com/Names_of_G-d/YHVH/ (accessed August 2013)

## Week 3

[1]Ibid, Brabson

[2]Logan, Jim. *Protecting Your Family from Spiritual Attacks: Reclaiming Surrendered Ground.* Chicago, IL: Moody Press, 1995.

[3]Daily, Jim with Stan Praimnath "As the Towers Were Falling" *Focus on the Family*. http://www.focus on the family.com/radio.aspx? ID+% (accessed September 11 2013).


## Week 4

[1]Vespie, Pastor Stan. *The Romance of Ruth*. Pastor Stan Vespie, 1998.

[2]Olsen, Rachel "God's Cleats-Encouragement for Today" *Crosswalk.com*. http://www.crosswalk.com/devotionals/encouragement/116266 68/print/ (accessed February 4 2010).


## Week 5

[1]DeHaan, M.R.. *The Tabernacle*. Grand Rapids, Michigan: Zondervan, 1983.

[2]Author Unknown "The Pearl Story" *MotivateUs.com*. http://www. motivateus.com/stories/pearls.html (accessed December 2012).

[3]VanderLaan, Ray. *Prophets and Kings. Faith Lessons on DVD*. Colorado Springs, Colorado: Focus on the Family, 2005.

[4]Ibid., Dehaan. *The Tabernacle*.


## Week 6

[1]Muller, George. *The Autobiography of George Muller*. Whitaker House, 1985.

Week 7

[1]DeHaan, M.R. *Broken Things: Why We Suffer.* Discovery House, 2009.

[2]Wiersbe, Warren. *Live Like A King.* Chicago, IL: The Moody Bible Institute of Chicago, 1993.

[3]Rozovsky, Lorne. "Jews and Shoes" *Chabad.org.* http://www.chabad.org/library/article-cdo/aid/407510/jewish/Jews-and-shoes.html (accessed September 26, 2013).

[4]"Echoes of Grace-How Great is His Beauty" *BibleTruth.com.* http://www.bibletruthpublishers.com/he-took-my-whipping-for-me/how-great-is-his-beauty/echoes-of-grace/la95573. (accessed September 7, 2013).

CPSIA information can be obtained
at www.ICGtesting.com
Printed in the USA
LVHW081454270520
656702LV00016B/480

9 781936 746842